JOYOUS GARD

JOYOUS GARD

ARTHUR CHRISTOPHER BENSON

WILDSIDE PRESS

JOYOUS GARD

Originally published in 1913.
This edition published in 2006 by Wildside Press, LLC.
www.wildsidepress.com

TO
ALL MY FRIENDS
KNOWN AND UNKNOWN
I DEDICATE THIS BOOK

PREFACE

It is a harder thing than it ought to be to write openly and frankly of things private and sacred. "Secretum meum mihi!" — "My secret is my own!" — cried St. Francis in a harrowed moment. But I believe that the instinct to guard and hoard the inner life is one that ought to be resisted. Secrecy seems to me now a very uncivilised kind of virtue, after all! We have all of us, or most of us, a quiet current of intimate thought, which flows on, gently and resistlessly, in the background of our lives, the volume and spring of which we cannot alter or diminish, because it rises far away at some unseen source, like a stream which flows through grassy pastures, and is fed by rain which falls on unknown hills from the clouds of heaven. This inner thought is hardly affected by the busy incidents of life — our work, our engagements, our public intercourse; but because it represents the self which we are always alone with, it makes up the greater part of our life, and is much more our real and true life than the life which we lead in public. It contains the things which we feel and hope, rather than what we say; and the fact that we do not speak our inner thoughts is what more than anything else keeps us apart from each other.

In this book I have said, or tried to say, just what I thought, and as I thought it; and since it is a book which recommends a studied quietness and a cheerful serenity of life, I have put my feelings to a vigorous test, by writing it, not when I was at ease and in leisure, but in the very thickest and fullest of my work. I thought that if the kind of quiet that I recommended had any force or weight at all, it should be the sort of quiet which I still could realise and value in a life full of engagements and duties and business, and that if it could be developed on a background of that kind, it might have a worth which it could not have if it were gently conceived in peaceful days and untroubled hours.

So it has all been written in spaces of hard-driven work, when the day never seemed long enough for all I had to do, between interruptions and interviews and teaching and meetings. But the sight and scent that I shall always connect with it, is that of a great lilac-bush which stands just outside my study window, and which day by day in this bright and chilly spring has held up its purple clusters, overtopping the dense, rich, pale foliage, against a blue and cloudless sky; and when the wind has been in the North, as it has often been, has filled my room with the scent of breaking buds. How often, as I wrote, have I cast a sidelong look at the lilac-bush! How often has it appeared to beckon me away from my papers to a freer and more fragrant air outside! But it seemed to me that I was perhaps obeying the call of the lilac best — though how far away from its freshness and sweetness! — if I tried to make my own busy life, which I do not pretend not to enjoy, break into such flower as it could, and give out what the old books call its 'spicery,' such as it is.

Because the bloom, the colour, the scent, are all there, if I could but express them. That is the truth! I do not claim to make them, to cause them, to create them, any more than the lilac could engender the scent of roses or of violets. Nor do I profess to do faithfully all that I say in my book that it is well to do. That is the worst, and yet perhaps it is the best, of books, that one presents in them one's hopes, dreams, desires, visions; more than one's dull and mean performances. 'Als ich kann!' That is the best one can do and say.

It is our own fault, and not the fault of our visions, that we cannot always say what we think in talk, even to our best friends. We begin to do so, perhaps, and we see a shadow gather. Either the friend does not understand, or he does not care, or he thinks it all unreal and affected; and then there falls on us a foolish shyness, and we become not what we are, but what we think the friend would like to think us; and so he 'gets to know' as he calls it, not what is really there, but what he chooses should be there.

But with pen in hand, and the blessed white paper before one, there is no need to be anything in the world but what one is. Our dignity must look after itself, and the dignity that we claim is worth nothing, especially if it is falsely claimed. But even the meanest flower that blows may claim to blossom as it can, and as indeed it must. In the democracy of flowers, even the dandelion has a right to a place, if it can find one, and to a vote, if it can get one; and even if it cannot, the wind is kind to it, and floats its arrowy down far afield, by wood and meadow, and into the unclaimed waste at last.

I
PRELUDE

The Castle of *Joyous Gard* in the *Morte D'Arthur* was Sir Lancelot's own castle, that he had won with his own hands. It was full of victual, and all manner of mirth and disport. It was hither that the wounded knight rode as fast as his horse might run, to tell Sir Lancelot of the misuse and capture of Sir Palamedes; and hence Lancelot often issued forth, to rescue those that were oppressed, and to do knightly deeds.

It was true that Lancelot afterwards named it *Dolorous Gard*, but that was because he had used it unworthily, and was cast out from it; but it recovered its old name again when they conveyed his body thither, after he had purged his fault by death. It was on the morning of the day when they set out, that the Bishop who had been with him when he died, and had given him all the rites that a Christian man ought to have, was displeased when they woke him out of his sleep, because, as he said, he was so merry and well at ease. And when they inquired the reason of his mirth, the Bishop said, "Here was Lancelot with me, with more angels than ever I saw men upon one day." So it was well with that great knight at the last!

I have called this book of mine by the name of *Joyous Gard*, because it speaks of a stronghold that we can win with our own hands, where we can abide in great content, so long as we are not careful to linger there in sloth and idleness, but are ready to ride abroad at the call for help. The only time in his life when Lancelot was deaf to that call, was when he shut himself up in the castle to enjoy the love that was his single sin. And it was that sin that cost him so dear, and lost the Castle its old and beautiful name. But when the angels made glad over the sinner who repented, as it is their constant use to do, and when it was only remembered of Lancelot that he had been a peerless knight, the name came back to the Castle; and that name is doubtless hidden now under some name of commoner use, whatever and wherever it may be.

In the *Pilgrim's Progress* we read how willing Mr. Interpreter was, in the House that was full of so many devices and surprises, to explain to the pilgrims the meaning of all the fantastic emblems and comfortable sights that he showed them. And I do not think it spoils a parable, but rather improves it, that it should have its secret meaning made plain.

The Castle of *Joyous Gard* then, which each of us can use, if we desire it, is the fortress of beauty and joy. We cannot walk into it by right, but must win it; and in a world like this, where there is much that is anxious and troublesome, we ought, if we can, to gain such a place, and provide it with all that we need, where we may have our seasons of rest and refreshment. It must not be idle and selfish joyance that we take there; it must be the interlude to toil and fight and painful deeds, and we must be ready to sally out in a moment when it is demanded of us. Now, if the winning of such a fortress of thought is hard, it is also dangerous when won, because it tempts us to immure ourselves in peace, and only observe from afar the plain of life, which lies all about the Castle, gazing down through the high windows; to shut out the wind and the rain, as well as the cries and prayers of those who have been hurt and dismayed by wrongful usage. If we do that, the day will come when we shall be besieged in our Castle, and ride away vanquished and disgraced, to do what we have neglected and forgotten.

But it is not only right, it is natural and wise, that we should have a stronghold in our minds, where we should frequent courteous and gentle and knightly company — the company of all who have loved beauty wisely and purely, such as poets and artists. Because we make a very great mistake if we allow the common course and use of the world to engulph us wholly. We must not be too dainty for the work of the world, but we may thankfully believe that it is only a mortal discipline, and that our true life is elsewhere, hid with God. If we grow to believe that life and its cares and business are all, we lose the freshness of life, just as we lose the strength of life if we reject its toil. But if we go at times to our *Joyous Gard*, we can bring back into common life something of the grace and seemliness and courtesy of the place. For the end of life is that we should do humble and common things in a fine and courteous manner, and mix with simple affairs, not condescendingly or disdainfully, but with all the eagerness and modesty of the true knight.

This little book then is an account, as far as I can give it, of what we may do to help ourselves in the matter, by feeding and nurturing the finer and sweeter thought, which, like all delicate things, often perishes from indifference and inattention. Those of us who are sensitive and imaginative and faint-hearted often miss our chance of better things by not forming plans and designs for our peace. We lament that we are hurried and pressed and occupied, and we cry,

"Yet, oh, the place could I but find!"

But that is because we expect to be conducted thither, without the trouble of the journey! Yet we can, like the wise King of Troy, build the walls of our castle to music, if we will, and see to the fit providing of the place; it only needs that we should set about it in earnest; and as I have often gratefully found that a single word of another can fall into the mind like a seed, and quicken to life while one sleeps, breaking unexpectedly into bloom, I will here say what comes into my mind to say, and point out the towers that I think I discern rising above the tangled forest, and glimmering tall and shapely and secure at the end of many an open avenue.

II
IDEAS

There are certain great ideas which, if we have any intelligence and thoughtfulness at all, we cannot help coming across the track of, just as when we walk far into the deep country, in the time of the blossoming of flowers, we step for a moment into a waft of fragrance, cast upon the air from orchard or thicket or scented field of bloom.

These ideas are very various in quality; some of them deliciously haunting and transporting, some grave and solemn, some painfully sad and strong. Some of them seem to hint at unseen beauty and joy, some have to do with problems of conduct and duty, some with the relation in which we wish to stand or are forced to stand with other human beings; some are questionings born of grief and pain, what the meaning of sorrow is, whether pain has a further intention, whether the spirit survives the life which is all that we can remember of existence; but the strange thing about all these ideas is that we find them suddenly in the mind and soul; we do not seem to invent them, though we cannot trace them; and even if we find them in books that we read or words that we hear, they do not seem wholly new to us; we recognise them as things that we have dimly felt and perceived, and the reason why they often have so mysterious an effect upon us is that they seem to take us outside of ourselves, further back than we can recollect, beyond the faint horizon, into something as wide and great as the illimitable sea or the depths of sunset sky.

Some of these ideas have to do with the constitution of society, the combined and artificial peace in which human beings live, and then they are political ideas; or they deal with such things as numbers, curves, classes of animals and plants, the soil of the earth, the changes of the seasons, the laws of weight and mass, and then they are scientific ideas; some have to do with right and wrong conduct, actions and qualities, and then they are religious or ethical ideas. But there is a class of thoughts which belong precisely to none of these things, but which are concerned with the perception of beauty, in forms and colours, musical sounds, human faces and limbs, words majestic or sweet; and this sense of beauty may go further, and may be discerned in qualities, regarded not from the point of view of their rightness and justice, but according as they are fine and noble, evoking our admiration and our desire; and these are poetical ideas.

It is not of course possible exactly to classify ideas, because there is a great overlapping of them and a wide interchange. The thought of the slow progress of man from something rude and beastlike, the statement of the astronomer about the swarms of worlds swimming in space, may awaken the sense of poetry which is in its essence the sense of wonder. I shall not attempt in these few pages to limit and define the sense of poetry. I shall merely attempt to describe the kind of effect it has or may have in life, what our relation is or may be to it, what claim it may be said to have upon us, whether we can practise it, and whether we ought to do so.

III

POETRY

I was reading the other day a volume of lectures delivered by Mr. Mackail at Oxford, as Professor of Poetry there. Mr. Mackail began by being a poet himself; he married the daughter of a great and poetical artist, Sir Edward Burne-Jones; he has written the *Life of William Morris*, which I think is one of the best biographies in the language, in its fine proportion, its seriousness, its vividness; and indeed all his writing has the true poetical quality. I hope he even contrives to communicate it to his departmental work in the Board of Education!

He says in the preface to his lectures, "Poetry is the controller of sullen care and frantic passion; it is the companion in youth of desire and love; it is the power which in later years dispels the ills of life — labour, penury, pain, disease, sorrow, death itself; it is the inspiration, from youth to age, and in all times and lands, of the noblest human motives and ardours, of glory, of generous shame, of freedom and the unconquerable mind."

In these fine sentences it will be seen that Mr. Mackail makes a very high and majestic claim indeed for poetry: no less than the claim of art, chivalry, patriotism, love, and religion all rolled into one! If that claim could be substantiated, no one in the world could be excused for not putting everything else aside and pursuing poetry, because it would seem to be both the cure for all the ills of life, and the inspirer of all high-hearted effort. It would be indeed the one thing needful!

But what I do not think Mr. Mackail makes quite clear is whether he means by poetry the expression in verse of all these great ideas, or whether he means a spirit much larger and mightier than what is commonly called poetry; which indeed only appears in verse at a single glowing point, as the electric spark leaps bright and hot between the coils of dark and cold wire.

I think it is a little confusing that he does not state more definitely what he means by poetry. Let us take another interesting and suggestive definition. It was Coleridge who said, "The opposite of poetry is not prose but science; the opposite of prose is not poetry but verse." That seems to me an even more fertile statement. It means that poetry is a certain sort of emotion, which may be gentle or vehement, but can be found both in verse and prose; and that its opposite is the unemotional classification of phenomena, the accurate statement of material laws; and that poetry is by no means the rhythmical and metrical expression of emotion, but emotion itself, whether it be expressed or not.

I do not wholly demur to Mr. Mackail's statement, if it may be held to mean that poetry is the expression of a sort of rapturous emotion, evoked by beauty, whether that beauty is seen in the forms and colours of earth, its gardens, fields, woods, hills, seas, its sky-spaces and sunset glories; or in the beauty of human faces and movements; or in noble endurance or generous action. For that is the one essential quality of poetry, that the thing or thought, whatever it is, should strike the mind as beautiful, and arouse in it that strange and wistful longing which beautiful things arouse. It is hard to define that longing, but it is essentially a desire, a claim to draw near to something desirable, to possess it, to be thrilled by it, to continue in it; the same emotion which made the apostle say at the sight of his Lord transfigured in glory, "Master, it is good for us to be here!"

Indeed we know very well what beauty is, or rather we have all within us a standard by which we can instinctively test the beauty of a sight or a sound; but it is not that we all agree about the beauty of different things. Some see a great deal more than others, and some eyes and ears are delighted and pleased by what to more trained and fastidious senses seems coarse and shocking and vulgar. But that makes little difference; the point is that we have within us an apprehension of a quality which gives us a peculiar kind of delight; and even if it does not give us that delight when we are dull or anxious or miserable, we still know that the quality is there. I remember how when I had a long and dreary illness, with much mental depression, one of my greatest tortures was to be for ever seeing the beauty in things, but not to be able to enjoy it. The part of the brain that enjoyed was sick and uneasy; but I was never in any doubt that beauty was there, and had power to please the soul, if only the physical machinery were not out of gear, so that the pain of transmission overcame the sense of delight.

Poetry is then in its essence the discerning of beauty; and that beauty is not only the beauty of things heard and seen, but may dwell very deep in the mind and soul, and be stirred by visions which seem to have no connection with outside things at all.

IV
POETRY AND LIFE

Now I will try to say how poetry enters into life for most of us; and this is not an easy thing to express, because one can only look into the treasure of one's own experience, wander through the corridors and halls of memory, and see the faded tapestries, the pictures, and, above all, the portraits which hang upon the walls. I suppose that there are many people into whose spirits poetry only enters in the form of love, when they suddenly see a face that they have beheld perhaps often before, and have vaguely liked, and realise that it has suddenly put on some new and delicate charm, some curve of cheek or floating tress; or there is something in the glance that was surely never there before, some consciousness of a secret that may be shared, some signal of half-alarmed interest, something that shows that the two lives, the two hearts, have some joyful significance for each other; and then there grows up that marvellous mood which men call love, which loses itself in hopes of meeting, in fears of coldness, in desperate desires to please, to impress; and there arise too all sorts of tremulous affections, which seem so petty, so absurd, and even so irritating, to the spectators of the awakening passion; desires to punish for the pleasure of forgiving, to withdraw for the joy of being recalled; a wild elated drama in which the whole world recedes into the background, and all life is merged for the lover in the half-sweet, half-fearful consciousness of one other soul,

> *Whose lightest whisper moves him more*
> *Than all the rangéd reasons of the world.*

And in this mood it is curious to note how inadequate common speech and ordinary language appear, to meet the needs of expression. Even young people with no literary turn, no gift of style, find their memory supplying for them all sorts of broken echoes and rhetorical phrases, picked out of half-forgotten romances; speech must be *soigneux* now, must be dignified, to meet so uplifting an experience. How oddly like a book the young lover talks, using so naturally the loud inflated phrases that seem so divorced from common-sense and experience! How common it is to see in law-reports, in cases which deal with broken engagements of marriage, to find in the excited letters which are read and quoted an irresistible tendency to drop into doggerel verse! It all seems to the sane reader such a grotesque kind of intoxication. Yet it is as natural as the airs and graces of the singing canary, the unfurling of the peacock's fan, the held breath and hampered strut of the turkey — a tendency to assume a greatness and a nobility that one does not possess, to seem impressive, tremendous, desirable. Ordinary talk will not do; it must rhyme, it must march, it must glitter, it must be stuck full of gems; accomplishments must be paraded, powers must be hinted at. The victor must advance to triumph with blown trumpets and beaten drums; and in solitude there must follow the reaction of despair, the fear that one has disgraced oneself, seemed clumsy and dull, done ignobly. Every sensitive emotion is awake; and even the most serene and modest natures, in the grip of passion, can become suspicious and self-absorbed, because the passion which consumes them is so fierce that it shrivels all social restraints, and leaves the soul naked, and bent upon the most uncontrolled self-emphasis.

But apart from this urgent passion, there are many quieter ways in which the same spirit, the same emotion, which is nothing but a sense of self-significance, comes into the soul. Some are so inspired by music, the combinations of melodies, the intricate conspiracy of chords and ordered vibrations, when the orchestra is at work, the great droning horns with their hollow reluctant voices sustaining the shiver and ripple of the strings; or by sweeter, simpler cadences played at evening, when the garden scents wafted out of the fragrant dusk, the shaded lamps, the listening figures, all weave themselves together into a mysterious tapestry of the sense, till we wonder what strange and beautiful scene is being enacted, and wherever we turn, catch hints and echoes of some bewildering and gracious secret, just not revealed!

Some find it in pictures and statues, the mellow liquid pageant of some old master-hand, a stretch of windspent moor, with its leaning grasses and rifted crags, a dark water among glimmering trees at twilight, a rich plain running to the foot of haze-hung mountains, the sharp-cut billows of a racing sea; or a statue with its shapely limbs and its veiled smile, or of the suspended strength of some struggling Titan: all these hold the same inexplicable appeal to the senses, indicating the efforts of spirits who have seen, and loved, and admired, and hoped, and desired, striving to leave some record of the joy that thrilled and haunted, and almost tortured them; and to many people the emotion comes most directly through the words and songs of poetry, that tell of joys lived through, and sorrows endured, of hopes that could not be satisfied, of desires that could not know fulfilment; pictures, painted in words, of scenes such as we ourselves have moved through in old moods of delight, scenes from which the marvellous alchemy of memory has abstracted all the base and dark elements, leaving only the pure gold of remembered happiness — the wide upland with the far-off plain, the garden flooded with sun, the grasses crisped with frost, the snow-laden trees, the flaming autumn woods, the sombre forest at shut of day, when the dusk creeps stealthily along the glimmering aisles, the stream passing clear among large-leaved water-plants and spires of bloom; and the mood goes deeper still, for it echoes the marching music of the heart, its glowing hopes, its longing for strength and purity and peace, its delight in the nearness of other hearts, its wisdom, its nobility.

But the end and aim of all these various influences is the same; their power lies in the fact that they quicken in the spirit the sense of the energy, the delight, the greatness of life, the share that we can claim in them, the largeness of our own individual hope and destiny; and that is the real work of all the thoughts that may be roughly called poetical; that they reveal to us something permanent and strong and beautiful, something which has an irrepressible energy, and which outlines itself clearly upon the dark background of days, a spirit with which we can join hands and hold deep communication, which we instinctively feel is the greatest reality of the world. In such moments we perceive that the times when we descend into the meaner and duller and drearier businesses of life are interludes in our real being, into which we have to descend, not because of the actual worth of the baser tasks, but that we may practise the courage and the hope we ought to bring away from the heavenly vision. The more that men have this thirst for beauty, for serene energy, for fulness of life, the higher they are in the scale, and the less will they quarrel with the obscurity and humility of their lives, because they are confidently waiting for a purer, higher, more untroubled life, to which we are all on our way, whether we realise it or no!

V

ART

It is not uncommon for me to receive letters from young aspirants, containing poems, and asking me for an opinion on their merits. Such a letter generally says that the writer feels it hardly worth while to go on writing poetry unless he or she is assured that the poems are worth something. In such cases I reply that the answer lies there! Unless it seems worth while, unless indeed poetry is the outcome of an irrepressible desire to express something, it is certainly not worth while writing. On the other hand, if the desire is there, it is just as well worth practising as any other form of artistic expression. A man who liked sketching in water-colours would not be restrained from doing so by the fear that he might not become an Academician, a person who liked picking out tunes on a piano need not desist because there is no prospect of his earning money by playing in public!

Poetry is of all forms of literary expression the least likely to bring a man credit or cash. Most intelligent people with a little gift of writing have a fair prospect of getting prose articles published. But no one wants third-rate poetry; editors fight shy of it, and volumes of it are unsaleable.

I have myself written so much poetry, have published so many volumes of verse, that I can speak sympathetically on the subject. I worked very hard indeed at poetry for seven or eight years, wrote little else, and the published volumes form only a small part of my output, which exists in many manuscript volumes. I achieved no particular success. My little books were fairly well received, and I sold a few hundred copies; I have even had a few pieces inserted in anthologies. But though I have wholly deserted the practice of poetry, and though I can by no means claim to be reckoned a poet, I do not in the least regret the years I gave to it. In the first place it was an intense pleasure to write. The cadences, the metres, the language, the rhymes, all gave me a rapturous delight. It trained minute observation — my poems were mostly nature-poems — and helped me to disentangle the salient points and beauties of landscapes, hills, trees, flowers, and even insects. Then too it is a very real training in the use of words; it teaches one what words are musical, sonorous, effective; while the necessity of having to fit words to metre increases one's stock of words and one's power of applying them. When I came back to writing prose, I found that I had a far larger and more flexible vocabulary than I had previously possessed; and though the language of poetry is by no means the same as that of prose — it is a pity that the two kinds of diction are so different in English, because it is not always so in other languages — yet it made the writing of ornamental and elaborate prose an easier matter; it gave one too a sense of form; a poem must have a certain balance and proportion; so that when one who has written verse comes to write prose, a subject falls easily into divisions, and takes upon itself a certain order of course and climax.

But these are only consequences and resulting advantages. The main reason for writing poetry is and must be the delight of doing it, the rapture of perceiving a beautiful subject, and the pleasure of expressing it as finely and delicately as one can. I have given it up because, as William Morris once said of himself, "to make poetry just for the sake of making it is a crime for a man of my age and experience!"

> *One's feelings lose poetic flow*
> *Soon after twenty-seven or so!*

One begins to think of experience in a different sort of way, not as a series of glowing points and pictures, which outline themselves radiantly upon a duller background, but as a rich full thing, like a great tapestry, all of which is important, if it is not all beautiful. It is not that the marvel and wonder of life is less; but it is more equable, more intricate, more mysterious. It does not rise at times, like a sea, into great crested breakers, but it comes marching in evenly, roller after roller, as far as the eye can reach.

And then too poetry becomes cramped and confined for all that one desires to say. One lived life, as a young man, rather for the sake of the emotions which occasionally transfigured it, with a priestly sense of its occasional splendour; there was not time to be leisurely, humorous, gently interested. But as we grow older, we perceive that poetical emotion is but one of many forces, and our sympathy grows and extends itself in more directions. One had but little patience in the old days for quiet, prosaic, unemotional people; but now it becomes clear that a great many persons live life on very simple and direct lines; one wants to understand their point of view better, one is conscious of the merits of plainer stuff; and so the taste broadens and deepens, and becomes like a brimming river rather than a leaping crystal fount. Life receives a hundred affluents, and is tinged with many new substances; and one begins to see that if poetry is the finest and sweetest interpretation of life, it is not always the completest or even the largest.

If we examine the lives of poets, we too often see how their inspiration flagged and failed. Milton indeed wrote his noblest verse in middle-age, after a life immersed in affairs. Wordsworth went on writing to the end, but all his best poetry was written in about five early years. Tennyson went on to a patriarchal age, but there is little of his later work that bears comparison with what he wrote before he was forty. Browning produced volume after volume, but, with the exception of an occasional fine lyric, his later work is hardly more than an illustration of his faults of writing. Coleridge deserted poetry very early; Byron, Shelley, Keats, all died comparatively young.

The Letters of Keats give perhaps a more vivid and actual view of the mind and soul of a poet than any other existing document. One sees there, naïvely and nobly expressed, the very essence of the poetical nature, the very soil out of which poetry flowers. It is wonderful, because it is so wholly sane, simple, and unaffected. It is usual to say that the Letters give one a picture of rather a second-rate and suburban young man, with vulgar friends and *banal* associations, with one prodigious and matchless faculty. But it is that very background that constitutes the supreme force of the appeal. Keats accepted his circumstances, his friends, his duties with a singular modesty. He was not for ever complaining that he was unappreciated and underestimated. His commonplaceness, when it appears, is not a defect of quality, but an eager human interest in the personalities among whom his lot was cast. But every now and then there swells up a poignant sense of passion and beauty, a sacred, haunting, devouring fire of inspiration, which leaps high and clear upon the homely altar.

Thus he writes: "This morning poetry has conquered — I have relapsed into those abstractions which are my only life — I feel escaped from a new, strange, and threatening sorrow. . . . There is an awful warmth about my heart, like a load of immortality." Or again: "I feel more and more every day, as my imagination strengthens, that I do not live in this world alone, but in a thousand worlds." And again: "I have loved the principle of beauty in all things."

One sees in these passages that there not only is a difference of force and passion, but an added quality of some kind in the mind of a poet, a combination of fine perception and emotion, which instantaneously and instinctively translates itself into words.

For it must never be forgotten how essential a part of the poet is the knack of words. I do not doubt that there are hundreds of people who are haunted and penetrated by a lively sense of beauty, whose emotions are fiery and sweet, but who have not just the intellectual store of words, which must drip like honey from an overflowing jar. It is a gift as definite as that of the sculptor or the musician, an exuberant fertility and swiftness of brain, that does not slowly and painfully fit a word into its place, but which breathes thought direct into music.

The most subtle account of this that I know is given in a passage in Shelley's *Defence of Poetry*. He says: "A man cannot say 'I will compose poetry' — the greatest poet even cannot say it; for the mind in creation is like a fading coal, which some invisible influence, like an inconstant wind, awakes to transitory brightness. The power arises from within, like the colour of a flower which fades and changes as it is developed, and the conscious portions of our nature are unprophetic either of its approach or its departure. When composition begins, inspiration is already on the decline."

That I believe is as true as it is beautiful. The best poetry is written in a sudden rapture, and probably needs but little reconsideration or retouching. One knows for instance how the *Ode to the Nightingale* was scribbled by Keats on a spring morning, in an orchard at Hampstead, and so little regarded that it was rescued by a friend from the volume into which he had crammed the slips of manuscript. Of course poets vary greatly in their method; but one may be sure of this, that no poem which was not a great poem in its first transcript, ever becomes a great poem by subsequent handling. There are poets indeed like Rossetti and FitzGerald who made a worse poem out of a better by scrupulous correction; and the first drafts of great poems are generally the finest poems of all. A poem has sometimes been improved by excision, notably in the case of Tennyson, whose abandoned stanzas, printed in his Life, show how strong his instinct was for what was best and purest. A great poet, for instance, never, like a lesser poet, keeps an unsatisfactory stanza for the sake of a good line. Tennyson, in a fine homely image, said that a poem must have a certain curve of its own, like the curve of the rind of a pared apple thrown on the floor. It must have a perfect evolution and progress, and this can sometimes be best arrived at by the omission of stanzas in which the inconstant or flagging mind turned aside from its design.

But it is certain that if the poet gets so much into the habit of writing poetry, that even when he has no sense of inspiration he must still write to satisfy a craving, the result will be worthless, as it too often was in the case of Wordsworth. Because such poems become literary instead of poetical; and literary poetry has no justification.

If we take a book like Rossetti's *House of Life*, we shall find that certain sonnets stand out with a peculiar freshness and brightness, as in the golden sunlight of an autumn morning; while many of the sonnets give us the sense of slow and gorgeous evolution, as if contrived by some poetical machine. I was interested to find, in studying the *House of Life* carefully, that all the finest poems are early work; and when I came to look at the manuscripts, I was rather horrified to see what an immense amount of alternatives had been produced. There would be, for instance, no less than eight or nine of those great slowly moving words, like 'incommunicable' or 'importunate' written down, not so much to express an inevitable idea as to fill an inevitable space; and thus the poems seem to lose their pungency by the slow absorption of painfully sought agglutinations of syllables, with a stately music of their own, of course, but garnered rather than engendered. Rossetti's great dictum about the prime necessity for poetry being 'fundamental brainwork' led him here into error. The brainwork must be fundamental and instinctive; it must all have been done before the poem is conceived; and very often a poet acquires his power through sacrificing elaborate compositions which have taught him certainty of touch, but are not in themselves great poetry. Subsequent brainwork often merely clouds the effect, and it was that on which Rossetti spent himself in vain.

The view which Keats took of his own *Endymion* is a far larger and bolder one. "I will write independently," he said. "I have written independently *without judgment*. I may write independently and *with judgment* hereafter. The genius of poetry must work out its own salvation in a man. It cannot be matured by law and precept, but by sensation and watchfulness in itself."

Of course, fine craftsmanship is an absolute necessity; but it is craftsmanship which is not only acquired by practice, but which is actually there from the first, just as Mozart, as a child of eight, could play passages which would tax the skill of the most accomplished virtuoso. It was not learnt by practice, that swift correspondence of eye and hand, any more than the little swallow learns to fly; it knows it all already, and is merely finding out what it knows.

And therefore there is no doubt that a man cannot become a poet by taking thought. He can perhaps compose impressive verse, but that is all. Poetry is, as Plato says, a divine sort of experience, some strange blending of inherited characteristics, perhaps the fierce emotion of some dumb ancestress combining with the verbal skill of some unpoetical forefather. The receipt is unknown, not necessarily unknowable.

Of course if one has poetry in one's soul, it is a tremendous temptation to desire its expression, because the human race, with its poignant desire for transfiguring visions, strews the path of the great poet with bays, and remembers him as it remembers no other human beings. What would one not give to interpret life thus, to flash the loveliness of perception into desirous minds, to set love and hope and yearning to music, to inspire anxious hearts with the sense that there is something immensely large, tender, and significant behind it all! That is what we need to be assured of — our own significance, our own share in the inheritance of joy; and a poet can teach us to wait, to expect, to arise, to adore, when the circumstances of our lives are wrapped in mist and soaked with dripping rain. Perhaps that is the greatest thing which poetry does for us, to reassure us, to enlighten us, to send us singing on our way, to bid us trust in God even though He is concealed behind calamity and disaster, behind grief and heaviness, misinterpreted to us by philosophers and priests, and horribly belied by the wrongful dealings of men.

VI
ART AND MORALITY

There is a perpetual debate going on — one of those moulting shuttlecocks that serve to make one's battledore give out a merry sound — about the relation of art to morals, and whether the artist or the poet ought to attempt to *teach* anything. It makes a good kind of debate, because it is conducted in large terms, to which the disputants attach private meanings. The answer is a very simple one. It is that art and morality are only beauty realised in different regions; and as to whether the artist ought to attempt to teach anything, that may be summarily answered by the simple dictum that no artist ought ever to attempt to teach anything, with which must be combined the fact that no one who is serious about anything can possibly help teaching, whether he wishes or no!

High art and high morality are closely akin, because they are both but an eager following of the law of beauty; but the artist follows it in visible and tangible things, and the moralist follows it in the conduct and relations of life. Artists and moralists must be for ever condemned to misunderstand each other, because the votary of any art cannot help feeling that it is the one thing worth doing in the world; and the artist whose soul is set upon fine hues and forms thinks that conduct must take care of itself, and that it is a tiresome business to analyse and formulate it; while the moralist who loves the beauty of virtue passionately, will think of the artist as a child who plays with his toys, and lets the real emotions of life go streaming past.

This is a subject upon which it is as well to hear the Greeks, because the Greeks were of all people who ever lived the most absorbingly interested in the problems of life, and judged everything by a standard of beauty. The Jews, of course, at least in their early history, had the same fiery interest in questions of conduct; but it would be as absurd to deny to Plato an interest in morals as to withhold the title of artist from Isaiah and the author of the Book of Job!

Plato, as is well known, took a somewhat whimsical view of the work of the poet. He said that he must exclude the poets from his ideal State, because they were the prophets of unreality. But he was thinking of a kind of man very different from the men whom we call poets. He thought of the poet as a man who served a patron, and tried to gloze over his patron's tyranny and baseness, under false terms of glory and majesty; or else he thought of dramatists, and considered them to be men who for the sake of credit and money played skilfully upon the sentimental emotions of ordinary people; and he fought shy of the writers who used tragic passions for the amusement of a theatre. Aristotle disagreed with Plato about this, and held that poetry was not exactly moral teaching, but that it disposed the mind to consider moral problems as interesting. He said that in looking on at a play, a spectator suffered, so to speak, by deputy, but all the same learned directly, if unconsciously, the beauty of virtue. When we come to our own Elizabethans, there is no evidence that in their plays and poetry they thought about morals at all. No one has any idea whether Shakespeare had any religion, or what it was; and he above all great writers that ever lived seems to have taken an absolutely impersonal view of the sins and affections of men and women. No one is scouted or censured or condemned in Shakespeare; one sees and feels the point of view of his villains and rogues; one feels with them that they somehow could hardly have done otherwise than they did; and to effect that is perhaps the crown of art.

But nowadays the poet, with whom one may include some few novelists, is really a very independent person. I am not now speaking of those who write basely and crudely, to please a popular taste. They have their reward; and after all they are little more than mountebanks, the end of whose show is to gather up pence in the ring.

But the poet in verse is listened to by few people, unless he is very great indeed; and even so his reward is apt to be intangible and scanty; while to be deliberately a lesser poet is perhaps the most unworldly thing that a man can do, because he thus courts derision; indeed, if there is a bad sign of the world's temper just now, it is that men will listen to politicians, scientists, men of commerce, and journalists, because these can arouse a sensation, or even confer material benefits; but men will not listen to poets, because they have so little use for the small and joyful thoughts that make up some of the best pleasures of life.

It is quite true, as I have said, that no artist ought ever deliberately to try to teach people, because that is not his business, and one can only be a good artist by minding one's business, which is to produce beautiful things; and the moment one begins to try to produce improving things, one goes off the line. But in England there has been of late a remarkable fusion of morality and art. Ruskin and Browning are clear enough proof that it is possible to be passionately interested in moral problems in an artistic way; while at the same time it is true, as I have said, that if any man cares eagerly for beauty, and does his best to present it, he cannot help teaching all those who are searching for beauty, and only require to be shown the way.

The work of all real teachers is to make great and arduous things seem simple and desirable and beautiful. A teacher is not a person who provides short-cuts to knowledge, or who only drills a character out of slovenly intellectual faults. The essence of all real teaching is a sort of inspiration. Take the case of a great teacher, like Arnold or Jowett; Arnold lit in his pupils' minds a kind of fire, which was moral rather than intellectual; Jowett had a power of putting a suggestive brilliancy into dull words and stale phrases, showing that they were but the crystallised formulas of ideas, which men had found wonderful or beautiful. The secret of such teaching is quite incommunicable, but it is a very high sort of art. There are many men who feel the inspiration of knowledge very deeply, and follow it passionately, who yet cannot in the least communicate the glow to others. But just as the great artist can paint a homely scene, such as we have seen a hundred times, and throw into it something mysterious, which reaches out hands of desire far beyond the visible horizon, so can a great teacher show that ideas are living things all bound up with the high emotions of men.

And thus the true poet, whether he writes verses or novels, is the greatest of teachers, not because he trains and drills the mind, but because he makes the thing he speaks of appear so beautiful and desirable that we are willing to undergo the training and drilling that are necessary to be made free of the secret. He brings out, as Plato beautifully said, "the beauty which meets the spirit like a breeze, and imperceptibly draws the soul, even in childhood, into harmony with the beauty of reason." The work of the poet then is "to elicit the simplest principles of life, to clear away complexity, by giving a glowing and flashing motive to live nobly and generously, to renew the unspoiled growth of the world, to reveal the secret hope silently hidden in the heart of man."

Renovabitur ut aquila juventus tua — thy youth shall be renewed as an eagle — that is what we all desire! Indeed it would seem at first sight that, to gain happiness, the best way would be, if one could, to prolong the untroubled zest of childhood, when everything was interesting and exciting, full of novelty and delight. Some few people by their vitality can retain that freshness of spirit all their life long. I remember how a friend of R. L. Stevenson told me, that Stevenson, when alone in London, desperately ill, and on the eve of a solitary voyage, came to see him; he himself was going to start on a journey the following day, and had to visit the lumber-room to get out his trunks; Stevenson begged to be allowed to accompany him, and, sitting on a broken chair, evolved out of the drifted accumulations of the place a wonderful romance. But that sort of eager freshness we most of us find to be impossible as we grow older; and we are confronted with the problem of how to keep care and dreariness away, how to avoid becoming mere trudging wayfarers, dully obsessed by all we have to do and bear. Can we not find some medicine to revive the fading emotion, to renew the same sort of delight in new thoughts and problems which we found in childhood in all unfamiliar things, to battle with the dreariness, the daily use, the staleness of life?

The answer is that it is possible, but only possible if we take the same pains about it that we take to provide ourselves with comforts, to save money, to guard ourselves from poverty. Emotional poverty is what we most of us have to dread, and we must make investments if we wish for revenues. We are many of us hampered, as I have said, by the dreariness and dulness of the education we receive. But even that is no excuse for sinking into melancholy bankruptcy, and going about the world full of the earnest capacity for woe, disheartened and disheartening.

A great teacher has the extraordinary power, not only of evoking the finest capacities from the finest minds, but of actually giving to second-rate minds a belief that knowledge is interesting and worth attention. What we have to do, if we have missed coming under the influence of a great teacher, is resolutely to put ourselves in touch with great minds. We shall not burst into flame at once perhaps, and the process may seem but the rubbing of one dry stick against another; one cannot prescribe a path, because we must advance upon the slender line of our own interests; but we can surely find some one writer who revives us and inspires us; and if we persevere, we find the path slowly broadening into a road, while the landscape takes shape and design around us. The one thing fortunately of which there is enough and to spare in the world is good advice, and if we find ourselves helpless, we can consult some one who seems to have a view of finer things, whose delight is fresh and eager, whose handling of life seems gracious and generous. It is as possible to do this, as to consult a doctor if we find ourselves out of health; and here we stiff and solitary Anglo-Saxons are often to blame, because we cannot bring ourselves to speak freely of these things, to be importunate, to ask for help; it seems to us at once impertinent and undignified; but it is this sort of dreary consideration, which is nothing but distorted vanity, and this still drearier dignity, which withholds from us so much that is beautiful.

    The one thing then that I wish to urge is that we should take up the pursuit in an entirely practical way; as Emerson said, with a splendid mixture of common sense and idealism, "hitch our waggon to a star." It is easy enough to lose ourselves in a vague sentimentalism, and to believe that only our cramped conditions have hindered us from developing into something very wonderful. It is easy too to drift into helpless materialism, and to believe that dulness is the natural lot of man. But the realm of thought is a very free citizenship, and a hundred doors will open to us if we only knock at them. Moreover, that realm is not like an over-populated country; it is infinitely large, and virgin soil; and we have only to stake out our claim; and then, if we persevere, we shall find that our *Joyous Gard* is really rising into the air about us — where else should we build our castles? — with all the glory of tower and gable, of curtain-wall and battlement, terrace and pleasaunce, hall and corridor; our own self-built paradise; and then perhaps the knight, riding lonely from the sunset woods, will turn in to keep us company, and the wandering minstrel will bring his harp; and we may even receive other visitors, like the three that stood beside the tent of Abraham in the evening, in the plain of Mamre, of whom no one asked the name or lineage, because the answer was too great for mortal ears to hear.

VII

INTERPRETATION

Is the secret of life then a sort of literary rapture, a princely thing, only possible through costly outlay and jealously selected hours, like a concert of stringed instruments, whose players are unknown, bursting on the ear across the terraces and foliaged walls of some enchanted garden? By no means! That is the shadow of the artistic nature, that the rare occasions of life, where sound and scent and weather and sweet companionship conspire together, are so exquisite, so adorable, that the votary of such mystical raptures begins to plan and scheme and hunger for these occasions, and lives in discontent because they arrive so seldom.

No art, no literature, are worth anything at all unless they send one back to life with a renewed desire to taste it and to live it. Sometimes as I sit on a sunny day writing in my chair beside the window, a picture of the box-hedge, the tall sycamores, the stone-tiled roof of the chapel, with the blue sky behind, globes itself in the lense of my spectacles, so entrancingly beautiful, that it is almost a disappointment to look out on the real scene. We like to see things mirrored thus and framed, we strangely made creatures of life; why, I know not, except that our finite little natures love to select and isolate experiences from the mass, and contemplate them so. But we must learn to avoid this, and to realise that if a particle of life, thus ordered and restricted, is beautiful, the thing itself is more beautiful still. But we must not depend helplessly upon the interpretations, the skilled reflections, of finer minds than our own. If we learn from a wise interpreter or poet the quality and worth of a fraction of life, it is that we may gain from him the power to do the same for ourselves elsewhere; we must learn to walk alone, not crave, like a helpless child, to be for ever led and carried in kindly arms. The danger of culture, as it is unpleasantly called, is that we get to love things because poets have loved them, and as they loved them; and there we must not stay; because we thus grow to fear and mistrust the strong flavours and sounds of life, the joys of toil and adventure, the desire of begetting, giving life, drawing a soul from the unknown; we come to linger in a half-lit place, where things reach us faintly mellowed, as in a vision, through enfolding trees and at the ends of enchanted glades. This book of mine lays no claim to be a pageant of all life's joys; it leaves many things untouched and untold; but it is a plea for this; that those who have to endure the common lot of life, who cannot go where they would, whose leisure is but a fraction of the day, before the morning's toil and after the task is done, whose temptation it is to put everything else away except food and sleep and work and anxiety, not liking life so but finding it so; — it is a plea that such as these should learn how experience, even under cramped conditions, may be finely and beautifully interpreted, and made rich by renewed intention. Because the secret lies hid in this, that we must observe life intently, grapple with it eagerly; and if we have a hundred lives before us, we can never conquer life till we have learned to ride above it, not welter helplessly below it. And the cramped and restricted life is all the grander for this, that it gives us a nobler chance of conquest than the free, liberal, wealthy, unrestrained life.

In the *Romaunt of the Rose* a little square garden is described, with its beds of flowers, its orchard-trees. The beauty of the place lies partly in its smallness, but more still in its running waters, its shadowy wells, wherein, as the writer says quaintly enough, are "*no frogs,*" and the conduit-pipes that make a "noise full-liking." And again in that beautiful poem of Tennyson's, one of his earliest, with the dew of the morning upon it, he describes *The Poet's Mind* as a garden:

> *In the middle leaps a fountain*
> *Like sheet lightning,*
> *Ever brightening*
> *With a low melodious thunder;*
> *All day and all night it is ever drawn*
> *From the brain of the purple mountain*
> *Which stands in the distance yonder:* . . .
> *And the mountain draws it from Heaven above,*
> *And it sings a song of undying love.*

That is a power which we all have, in some degree, to draw into our souls, or to set running through them, the streams of Heaven — for like water they will run in the dullest and darkest place if only they be led thither; and the lower the place, the stronger the stream! I am careful not to prescribe the source too narrowly, for it must be to our own liking, and to our own need. And so I will not say "love this and that picture, read this and that poet!" because it is just thus, by following direction too slavishly, that we lose our own particular inspiration. Indeed I care very little about fineness of taste, fastidious critical rejections, scoffs and sneers at particular fashions and details. One knows the epicure of life, the man who withdraws himself more and more from the throng, cannot bear to find himself in dull company, reads fewer and fewer books, can hardly eat and drink unless all is exactly what he approves; till it becomes almost wearisome to be with him, because it is such anxious and scheming work to lay out everything to please him, and because he will never take his chance of anything, nor bestir himself to make anything out of a situation which has the least commonness or dulness in it. Of course only with the command of wealth is such life possible; but the more delicate such a man grows, the larger and finer his maxims become, and the more he casts away from his philosophy the need of practising anything. One must think, such men say, clearly and finely, one must disapprove freely, one must live only with those whom one can admire and love; till they become at last like one of those sad ascetics, who spent their time on the top of pillars, and for ever drew up stones from below to make the pillar higher yet.

One is at liberty to mistrust whatever makes one isolated and superior; not of course that one's life need be spent in a sort of diffuse sociability; but one must practise an ease that is never embarrassed, a frankness that is never fastidious, a simplicity that is never abashed; and behind it all must spring the living waters, with the clearness of the sky and the cleanness of the hill about them, running still swiftly and purely in our narrow garden-ground, and meeting the kindred streams that flow softly in many other glad and desirous hearts.

In the beautiful old English poem, *The Pearl*, where the dreamer seems to be instructed by his dead daughter Marjory in the heavenly wisdom, she tells him that "all the souls of the blest are equal in happiness — that they are all kings and queens." [See Professor W. P. Ker's *English Literature, Mediæval*, p. 194.]

That is a heavenly kind of kingship, when there are none to be ruled or chidden, none to labour and serve; but it means the fine frankness and serenity of mind which comes of kingship, the perfect ease and dignity which springs from not having to think of dignity or pre-eminence at all.

Long ago I remember how I was sent for to talk with Queen Victoria in her age, and how much I dreaded being led up to her by a majestic lord-in-waiting; she sate there, a little quiet lady, so plainly dressed, so simple, with her hands crossed on her lap, her sanguine complexion, her silvery hair, yet so crowned with dim history and tradition, so great as to be beyond all pomp or ceremony, yet wearing the awe and majesty of race and fame as she wore her plain dress. She gave me a little nod and smile, and began at once to talk in the sweet clear voice that was like the voice of a child. Then came my astonishment. She knew, it seemed, all about me and my doings, and the doings of my relations and friends — not as if she had wished to be prepared to surprise me; but because her motherly heart had wanted to know, and had been unable to forget. The essence of that charm, which flooded all one's mind with love and loyalty, was not that she was great, but that she was entirely simple and kind; because she loved, not her great part in life, but life itself.

That kingship and queenship is surely not out of the reach of any of us; it depends upon two things: one, that we keep our minds and souls fresh with the love of life, which is the very dew of heaven; and the other that we claim not rights but duties, our share in life, not a control over it; if all that we claim is not to rule others, but to be interested in them, if we will not be shut out from love and care, then the sovereignty is in sight, and the nearer it comes the less shall we recognise it; for the only dignity worth the name is that which we do not know to be there.

VIII
EDUCATION

It is clear that the progress of the individual and the world alike depends upon the quickening of ideas. All civilisation, all law, all order, all controlled and purposeful life, will be seen to depend on these ideas and emotions. The growing conception of the right of every individual to live in some degree of comfort and security is nothing but the taking shape of these ideas and emotions; for the end of all civilisation is to ensure that there shall be freedom for all from debasing and degrading conditions, and that is perhaps as far as we have hitherto advanced; but the further end in sight is to set all men and women free to some extent from hopeless drudgery, to give them leisure, to provide them with tastes and interests; and further still, to contrive, if possible, that human beings shall not be born into the world of tainted parentage, and thus to stamp out the tyranny of disease and imbecility and criminal instinct. More and more does it become clear that all the off-scourings and failures of civilisation are the outcome of diseased brains and nerves, and that self-control and vigour are the results of nature rather than nurture. All this is now steadily in sight. The aim is personal freedom, the freedom which shall end where another's freedom begins; but we recognise now that it is no use legislating for social and political freedom, if we allow the morally deficient to beget offspring for whom moral freedom is an impossibility. And perhaps the best hope of the race lies in firmly facing this problem.

But, as I say, we have hardly entered upon this stage. We have to deal with things as they are, with many natures tainted by moral feebleness, by obliquity of vision, by lack of proportion. The hope at present lies in the endeavour to find some source of inspiration, in a determination not to let men and women grow up with fine emotions atrophied; and here the whole system of education is at fault. It is all on the lines of an intellectual gymnastic; little or nothing is done to cultivate imagination, to feed the sense of beauty, to arouse interest, to awaken the sleeping sense of delight. There is no doubt that all these emotions are dormant in many people. One has only to reflect on the influence of association, to know how children who grow up in a home atmosphere which is fragrant with beautiful influences, generally carry on those tastes and habits into later life. But our education tends neither to make men and women efficient for the simple duties of life, nor to arouse the gentler energies of the spirit. "You must remember you are translating poetry," said a conscientious master to a boy who was construing Virgil. "It's not poetry when I translate it!" said the boy. I look back at my own schooldays, and remember the bare, stately class-rooms, the dry wind of intellect, the dull murmur of work, neither enjoyed nor understood; and I reflect how small a part any fanciful or beautiful or leisurely interpretation ever played in our mental exercises; the first and last condition of any fine sort of labour — that it should be enjoyed — was put resolutely out of sight, not so much as an impossible adjunct, as a thing positively enervating and contemptible. Yet if one subtracts the idea of enjoyment from labour, there is no beauty-loving spirit which does not instantly and rightly rebel. There must be labour, of course, effective, vigorous, brisk labour, overcoming difficulties, mastering uncongenial details; but the end should be enjoyment; and it should be made clear that the greater the mastery, the richer the enjoyment; and that if one cannot enjoy a thing without mastering it, neither can one ever really master it without enjoying it.

What we need, in education, is some sense of far horizons and beautiful prospects, some consciousness of the largeness and mystery and wonder of life. To take a simple instance, in my own education. I read the great books of Greece and Rome; but I knew hardly anything of the atmosphere, the social life, the human activity out of which they proceeded. One did not think of the literature of the Greeks as of a fountain of eager beauty springing impulsively and instinctively out of the most ardent, gracious, sensitive life that any nation has ever lived. One knew little of the stern, businesslike, orderly, grasping Roman temperament, in which poetry flowered so rarely, and the arts not at all, until the national fibre began to weaken and grow dissolute. One studied history in those days, as if one was mastering statute-books, blue-books, gazettes, office-files; one never grasped the clash of individualities, or the real interests and tastes of the nations that fought and made laws and treaties. It was all a dealing with records and monuments, just the things that happened to survive decay — as though one's study of primitive man were to begin and end with sharpened flints!

What we have now to do, in this next generation, is not to leave education a dry conspectus of facts and processes, but to try rather that children should learn something of the temper and texture of the world at certain vivid points of its history; and above all perceive something of the nature of the world as it now is, its countries, its nationalities, its hopes, its problems. That is the aim, that we should realise what kind of a thing life is, how bright and yet how narrow a flame, how bounded by darkness and mystery, and yet how vivid and active within its little space of sun.

IX
KNOWLEDGE

"Knowledge is power," says the old adage; and yet so meaningless now, in many respects, do the words sound, that it is hard even to recapture the mental outlook from which it emanated. I imagine that it dates from a time when knowledge meant an imagined acquaintance with magical secrets, short cuts to wealth, health, influence, fame. Even now the application of science to the practical needs of man has some semblance of power about it; the telephone, wireless telegraphy, steam engines, anæsthetics — these are powerful things. But no man is profited by his discoveries; he cannot keep them to himself, and use them for his own private ends. The most he can do is to make a large fortune out of them. And as to other kinds of knowledge, erudition, learning, how do they profit the possessor? "No one knows anything nowadays," said an eminent man to me the other day; "it is not worth while! The most learned man is the man who knows best where to find things." There still appears, in works of fiction, with pathetic persistence, a belief that learning still lingers at Oxford and Cambridge; those marvellous Dons, who appear in the pages of novels, men who read folios all the morning and drink port all the evening, where are they in reality? Not at Cambridge, certainly. I would travel many miles, I would travel to Oxford, if I thought I could find such an adorable figure. But the Don is now a brisk and efficient man of business, a paterfamilias with provision to make for his family. He has no time for folios and no inclination for port. Examination papers in the morning, and a glass of lemonade at dinner, are the notes of his leisure days. The belief in uncommercial knowledge has indeed died out of England. Eton, as Mr. Birrell said, can hardly be described as a place of education; and to what extent can Oxford and Cambridge be described as places of literary research? A learned man is apt to be considered a bore, and the highest compliment that can be paid him is that one would not suspect him of being learned.

There is, indeed, a land in which knowledge is respected, and that is America. If we do not take care, the high culture will desert our shores, like Astræa's flying hem, and take her way Westward, with the course of Empire.

A friend of mine once told me that he struggled up a church-tower in Florence, a great lean, pale brick minaret, designed, I suppose, to be laminated with marble, but cheerfully abandoned to bareness; he came out on to one of those high balustraded balconies, which in mediæval pictures seem to have been always crowded with fantastically dressed persons, and are now only visited by tourists. The silvery city lay outspread beneath him, with the rapid mud-stained river passing to the plain, the hill-side crowded with villas embowered in green gardens, and the sad-coloured hills behind. While he was gazing, two other tourists, young Americans, came quietly out on to the balcony, a brother and sister, he thought. They looked out for a time in silence, leaning on the parapet; and then the brother said softly, "How much we should enjoy all this, if we were not so ignorant!" Like all Americans, they wanted to know! It was not enough for them to see the high houses, the fantastic towers, the great blind blocks of mediæval palaces, thrust so grimly out above the house-tops. It all meant life and history, strife and sorrow, it all needed interpreting and transfiguring and re-peopling; without that it was dumb and silent, vague and bewildering. One does not know whether to admire or to sigh! Ought one not to be able to take beauty as it comes? What if one does not want to know these things, as Shelley said to his lean and embarrassed tutor at Oxford? If knowledge makes the scene glow and live, enriches it, illuminates it, it is well. And perhaps in England we learn to live so incuriously and naturally among historical things that we forget the existence of tradition, and draw it in with the air we breathe, just realising it as a pleasant background and not caring to investigate it or master it. It is hard to say what we lose by ignorance, is hard to say what we should gain by knowledge. Perhaps to want to know would be a sign of intellectual and emotional activity; but it could not be done as a matter of duty — only as a matter of enthusiasm.

The poet Clough once said, "It makes a great difference to me that Magna Charta was signed at Runnymede, but it does not make much difference to me to know that it was signed." The fact that it was so signed affects our liberties, the knowledge only affects us, if it inspires us to fresh desire of liberty, whatever liberty may be. It is even more important to be interested in life than to be interested in past lives. It was Scott, I think, who asked indignantly,

> *Lives there the man with soul so dead,*
> *Who never to himself hath said*
> *This is my own, my native land?*

I do not know how it may be in Scotland! Dr. Johnson once said rudely that the finest prospect a Scotchman ever saw was the high road that might take him to England; but I should think that if

Scott's is a fair test of deadness of soul, there must be a good many people in England who are as dead as door-nails! The Englishman is not very imaginative; and a farmer who was accustomed to kneel down like Antæus, and kiss the soil of his orchard, would be thought an eccentric!

Shall we then draw a cynical conclusion from all this, and say that knowledge is a useless burden; or if we think so, why do we think it? I have very little doubt in my own mind that why so many young men despise and even deride knowledge is because knowledge has been presented to them in so arid a form, so little connected with anything that concerns them in the remotest degree. We ought, I think, to wind our way slowly back into the past from the present; we ought to start with modern problems and modern ideas, and show people how they came into being; we ought to learn about the world, as it is, first, and climb the hill slowly. But what we do is to take the history of the past, Athens and Rome and Judæa, three glowing and shining realms, I readily admit; but we leave the gaps all unbridged, so that it seems remote, abstruse, and incomprehensible that men should ever have lived and thought so.

Then we deluge children with the old languages, not teaching them to read, but to construe, and cramming the little memories with hideous grammatical forms. So the whole process of education becomes a dreary wrestling with the uninteresting and the unattainable; and when we have broken the neck of infantile curiosity with these uncouth burdens, we wonder that life becomes a place where the only aim is to get a good appointment, and play as many games as possible.

Yet learning need not be so cumbrously carried after all! I was reading a few days ago a little book by Professor Ker, on mediæval English, and reading it with a species of rapture. It all came so freshly and pungently out of a full mind, penetrated with zest and enjoyment. One followed the little rill of literary craftsmanship so easily out of the plain to its high source among the hills, till I wondered why on earth I had not been told some of these delightful things long ago, that I might have seen how our great literature took shape. Such scraps of knowledge as I possess fell into shape, and I saw the whole as in a map outspread.

And then I realised that knowledge, if it was only rightly directed, could be a beautiful and attractive thing, not a mere fuss about nothing, dull facts reluctantly acquired, readily forgotten.

All children begin by wanting to know, but they are often told not to be tiresome, which generally means that the elder person has no answer to give, and does not like to appear ignorant. And then the time comes for Latin Grammar, and Cicero de Senectute, and Cæsar's Commentaries, and the bewildered stripling privately resolves to have no more than he can help to do with these antique horrors. The marvellous thing seems to him to be that men of flesh and blood could have found it worth their while to compose such things.

Erudition, great is thy sin! It is not that one wants to deprive the savant of his knowledge; one only wants a little common-sense and imaginative sympathy. How can a little boy guess that some of the most beautiful stories in the world lie hid among a mass of wriggling consonants, or what a garden lurks behind the iron gate, with βλωσκω and μολουμαι to guard the threshold?

I am not going here to discuss the old curriculum. "Let 'em 'ave it!" as the parent said to the schoolmaster, under the impression that it was some instrument of flagellation — as indeed it is, I look round my book-lined shelves, and reflect how much of interest and pleasure those parallel rows have meant to me, and how I struggled into the use of them outside of and not because of my so-called education; and how much they might mean to others if they had not been so conscientiously bumped into paths of peace.

"Nothing," said Pater, speaking of art in one of his finest passages, "nothing which has ever engaged the great and eager affections of men and women can ever wholly lose its charm." Not to the initiated, perhaps! But I sometimes wonder if anything which has been taught with dictionary and grammar, with parsing and construing, with detention and imposition, can ever wholly regain its charm. I am afraid that we must make a clean sweep of the old processes, if we have any intention of interesting our youth in the beauty of human ideas and their expression. But while we do not care about beauty and interest in life, while we conscientiously believe, in spite of a cataract of helpless facts, in the virtues of the old grammar-grind, so long shall we remain an uncivilised nation. Civilisation does not consist in commercial prosperity, or even in a fine service of express trains. It resides in quick apprehension, lively interest, eager sympathy . . . at least I suspect so.

"Like a crane or a swallow, so did I chatter!" said the rueful prophet. I do not write as a pessimist, hardly as a critic; still less as a censor; to waste time in deriding others' theories of life is a very poor substitute for enjoying it! I think we do very fairly well as we are; only do not let us indulge in the cant in which educators so freely indulge, the claim that we are interested in ideas intellectual or artistic, and that we are trying to educate our youth in these things. We do produce some intellectual athletes, and we knock a few hardy minds more or less into shape; but meanwhile a great river of opportunities, curiosity, intelligence, taste, interest, pleasure, goes idly weltering, through mud-flats and lean promontories and bare islands to the sea. It is the loss, the waste, the folly, of it that I deplore.

X
GROWTH

As the years go on, what one begins to perceive about so many people — though one tries hard to believe it is not so — is that somehow or other the mind does not grow, the view does not alter; life ceases to be a pilgrimage, and becomes a journey, such as a horse takes in a farm-cart. He is pulling something, he has got to pull it, he does not care much what it is — turnips, hay, manure! If he thinks at all, he thinks of the stable and the manger. The middle-aged do not try experiments, they lose all sense of adventure. They make the usual kind of fortification for themselves, pile up a shelter out of prejudices and stony opinions. It is out of the wind and rain, and the prospect is safely excluded. The landscape is so familiar that the entrenched spirit does not even think about it, or care what lies behind the hill or across the river.

Now of course I do not mean that people can or should play fast and loose with life, throw up a task or a position the moment they are bored with it, be at the mercy of moods. I am speaking here solely of the possible adventures of mind and soul; it is good, wholesome, invigorating, to be tied to a work in life, to have to discharge it whether one likes it or no, through indolence and disinclination, through depression and restlessness. But we ought not to be immured among conventions and received opinions. We ought to ask ourselves why we believe what we take for granted, and even if we do really believe it at all. We ought not to condemn people who do not move along the same lines of thought; we ought to change our minds a good deal, not out of mere levity, but because of experience. We ought not to think too much of the importance of what we are doing, and still less of the importance of what we have done; we ought to find a common ground on which to meet distasteful people; we ought to labour hard against self-pity as well as against self-applause; we ought to feel that if we have missed chances, it is out of our own heedlessness and stupidity. Self-applause is a more subtle thing even than self-pity, because, if one rejects the sense of credit, one is apt to congratulate oneself on being the kind of person who does reject it, whereas we ought to avoid it as instinctively as we avoid a bad smell. Above all, we ought to believe that we can do something to change ourselves, if we only try; that we can anchor our conscience to a responsibility or a personality, can perceive that the society of certain people, the reading of certain books, does affect us, make our mind grow and germinate, give us a sense of something fine and significant in life. The thing is to say, as the prim governess says in Shirley, "You acknowledge the inestimable worth of principle?" — it is possible to get and to hold a clear view, as opposed to a muddled view, of life and its issues; and the blessing is that one can do this in any circle, under any circumstances, in the midst of any kind of work. That is the wonderful thing about thought, that it is like a captive balloon which is anchored in one's garden. It is possible to climb into it and to cast adrift; but so many people, as I have said, seem to end by pulling the balloon in, letting out the gas, and packing the whole away in a shed. Of course the power of doing all this varies very much in different temperaments; but I am sure that there are many people who, looking back at their youth, are conscious that they had something stirring and throbbing within them which they have somehow lost; some vision, some hope, some faint and radiant ideal. Why do they lose it, why do they settle down on the lees of life, why do they snuggle down among comfortable opinions? Mostly, I am sure, out of a kind of indolence. There are a good many people who say to themselves, "After all, what really matters is a solid defined position in the world; I must make that for myself, and meanwhile I must not indulge myself in any fancies; it will be time to do that when I have earned my pension and settled my children in life." And then when the time arrives, the frail and unsubstantial things are all dead and cannot be recovered; for happiness cannot be achieved along these cautious and heavy lines.

And so I say that we must deliberately aim at something different from the first. We must not block up the further views and wider prospects; we must keep the horizon open. What I here suggest has nothing whatever that is unpractical about it; it is only a deeper foresight, a more prudent wisdom. We must say to ourselves that whatever happens, the soul shall not be atrophied; and we should be as anxious about it, if we find that it is losing its zest and freedom, as we should be if we found that the body were losing its appetite!

It is no metaphor then, but sober earnest, when I say that when we take our place in the working world, we ought to lay the foundations of that other larger stronghold of the soul, *Joyous Gard*. All that matters is that we should choose a fair site for it in free air and beside still waters; and that we should plan it for ourselves, set out gardens and plantations, with as large a scheme as we can make for it, expecting the grace and greenery that shall be, and the increase which God gives. It may be that we shall have to build it slowly, and we may have to change the design many times; but it will be all built out of our own mind and hope, as the nautilus evolves its shell.

I am not speaking of a scheme of self-improvement, of culture followed that it may react on our profession or bring us in touch with useful people, of mental discipline, of correct information. The *Gard* is not to be a factory or an hotel; it must be frankly built *for our delight*. It is delight that we must follow, everything that brims the channel of life, stimulates, freshens, enlivens, tantalises, attracts. It must at all costs be beautiful. It must embrace that part of religion that glows for us, the thing which we find beautiful in other souls, the art, the poetry, the tradition, the love of nature, the craft, the interests we hanker after. It need not contain all these things, because we can often do better by checking diffuseness, and by resolute self-limitation. It is not by believing in particular books, pictures, tunes, tastes, that we can do it. That ends often as a mere prison to the thought; it is rather by meeting the larger spirit that lies behind life, recognising the impulse which meets us in a thousand forms, which forces us not to be content with narrow and petty things, but emerges as the energy, whatever it is, that pushes through the crust of life, as the flower pushes through the mould. Our dulness, our acquiescence in monotonous ways, arise from our not realising how infinitely important that force is, how much it has done for man, how barren life is without it. Here in England many of us have a dark suspicion of all that is joyful, inherited perhaps from our Puritan ancestry, a fear of yielding ourselves to its influence, a terror of being grimly repaid for indulgence, an old superstitious dread of somehow incurring the wrath of God, if we aim at happiness at all. We must know, many of us, that strange shadow which falls upon us when we say, "I feel so happy today that some evil must be going to befal me!" It is true that afflictions must come, but they are not to spoil our joy; they are rather to refine it and strengthen it. And those who have yielded themselves to joy are often best equipped to get the best out of sorrow.

We must aim then at fulness of life; not at husbanding our resources with meagre economy, but at spending generously and fearlessly, grasping experience firmly, nurturing zest and hope. The frame of mind we must be beware of, which is but a stingy vanity, is that which makes us say, "I am sure I should not like that person, that book, that place!" It is that closing-in of our own possibilities that we must avoid.

There is a verse in the Book of Proverbs that often comes into my mind; it is spoken of a reprobate, whose delights indeed are not those that the soul should pursue; but the temper in which he is made to cling to the pleasure which he mistakes for joy, is the temper, I am sure, in which one should approach life. He cries, *"They have stricken me, and I was not sick; they have beaten me, and I felt it not. When shall I awake? I will seek it yet again."*

XI

EMOTION

We are a curious nation, we English! Stendhal says that our two most patent vices are bashfulness and cant. That is to say, we are afraid to say what we think, and when we have gained the courage to speak, we say more than we think. We are really an emotional nation at heart, easily moved and liking to be moved; we are largely swayed by feeling, and much stirred by anything that is picturesque. But we are strangely ashamed of anything that seems like sentiment; and so far from being bluff and unaffected about it, we are full of the affectation, the pretence of not being swayed by our emotions. We have developed a curious idea of what men and women ought to be; and one of our pretences is that men should affect not to understand sentiment, and to leave, as we rudely say, "all that sort of thing to the women." Yet we are much at the mercy of clap-trap and mawkish phrases, and we like rhetoric partly because we are too shy to practise it. The result of it is that we believe ourselves to be a frank, outspoken, good-natured race; but we produce an unpleasant effect of stiffness, angularity, discourtesy, and self-centredness upon more genial nations. We defend our bluffness by believing that we hold emotion to be too rare and sacred a quality to be talked about, though I always have a suspicion that if a man says that a subject is too sacred to discuss, he probably also finds it too sacred to think about very much either; yet if one can get a sensible Englishman to talk frankly and unaffectedly about his feelings, it is often surprising to find how delicate they are.

One of our chief faults is our love of property, and the consequence of that is our admiration for what we call "businesslike" qualities. It is really from the struggle between the instinct of possession and the emotional instinct that our bashfulness arises; we are afraid of giving ourselves away, and of being taken advantage of; we value position and status and respectability very high; we like to know who a man is, what he stands for, what his influence amounts to, what he is worth; and all this is very injurious to our simplicity, because we estimate people so much not by their real merits but by their accumulated influence. I do not believe that we shall ever rise to true greatness as a nation until we learn not to take property so seriously. It is true that we prosper in the world at present, we keep order, we make money, we spread a bourgeois sort of civilisation, but it is not a particularly fine or fruitful civilisation, because it deals so exclusively with material things. I do not wish to decry the race, because it has force, toughness, and fine working qualities; but we do not know what to do with our prosperity when we have got it; we can make very little use of leisure; and our idea of success is to have a well-appointed house, expensive amusements, and to distribute a dull and costly hospitality, which ministers more to our own satisfaction than to the pleasure of the recipients.

There really can be few countries where men are so contented to be dull! There is little speculation or animation or intelligence or interest among us, and people who desire such an atmosphere are held to be fanciful, eccentric, and artistic. It was not always so with our race. In Elizabethan times we had all the inventiveness, the love of adventure, the pride of dominance that we have now; but there was then a great interest in things of the mind as well, a lively taste for ideas, a love of beautiful things and thoughts. The Puritan uprising knocked all that on the head, but Puritanism was at least preoccupied with moral ideas, and developed an excitement about sin which was at all events a sign of intellectual ferment. And then we did indeed decline into a comfortable sort of security, into a stale classical tradition, with pompous and sonorous writing on the one hand, and with neatness, literary finish, and wit rather than humour on the other. That was a dull, stolid, dignified time; and it was focussed into a great figure of high genius, filled with the combative common-sense which Englishmen admire, the figure of Dr. Johnson. His influence, his temperament, portrayed in his matchless biography, did indeed dominate literary England to its hurt; because the essence of Johnson was his freshness, and in his hands the great rolling Palladian sentences contrived to bite and penetrate; but his imitators did not see that freshness was the one requisite; and so for a generation the pompous rotund tradition flooded English prose; but for all that, England was saved in literature from mere stateliness by the sudden fierce interest in life and its problems which burst out like a spring in eighteenth-century fiction; and so we come to the Victorian era, when we were partially submerged by prosperity, scientific invention, commerce, colonisation. But the great figures of the century arose and had their say — Carlyle, Tennyson, Browning, Ruskin, William Morris; it was there all the time, that spirit of fierce hope and discontent and emotion, that deep longing to penetrate the issues and the significance of life.

It may be that the immense activity of science somewhat damped our interest in beauty; but that is probably a temporary thing. The influence exerted by the early scientists was in the direction of facile promises to solve all mysteries, to analyse everything into elements, to classify, to track out natural laws; and it was believed that the methods and processes of life would be divested of their secrecy and their irresponsibility; but the effect of further investigation is to reveal that life is infinitely more complex than was supposed, and that the end is as dim as ever; though science did for a while make havoc of the stereotyped imaginative systems of faith and belief, so that men supposed that beauty was but an accidental emphasis of law, and that the love of it could be traced to very material preferences.

The artist was for a time dismayed, at being confronted by the chemist who held that he had explained emotion because he had analysed the substance of tears; and for a time the scientific spirit drove the spirit of art into cliques and coteries, so that artists were hidden, like the Lord's prophets, by fifties in caves, and fed upon bread and water.

What mostly I would believe now injures and overshadows art, is that artists are affected by the false standard of prosperous life, are not content to work in poverty and simplicity, but are anxious, as all ambitious natures who love applause must be, to share in the spoils of the Philistines. There are, I know, craftsmen who care nothing at all for these things, but work in silence and even in obscurity at what seems to them engrossing and beautiful; but they are rare; and when there is so much experience and pleasure and comfort abroad, and when security and deference so much depend upon wealth, the artist desires wealth, more for the sake of experience and pleasure than for the sake of accumulation.

But the spirit which one desires to see spring up is the Athenian spirit, which finds its satisfaction in ideas and thoughts and beautiful emotions, in mental exploration and artistic expression; and is so absorbed, so intent upon these things that it can afford to let prosperity flow past like a muddy stream. Unfortunately, however, the English spirit is solitary rather than social, and the artistic spirit is jealous rather than inclusive; and so it comes about that instead of artists and men of ideas consorting together and living a free and simple life, they tend to dwell in lonely fortresses and paradises, costly to create, costly to maintain. The English spirit is against communities. If it were not so, how easy it would be for people to live in groups and circles, with common interests and tastes, to encourage each other to believe in beautiful things, and to practise ardent thoughts and generous dreams. But this cannot be done artificially, and the only people who ever try to do it are artists, who do occasionally congregate in a place, and make no secret to each other of what they are pursuing. I have sometimes touched the fringe of a community like that, and have been charmed by the sense of a more eager happiness, a more unaffected intercourse of spirits than I have found elsewhere. But the world intervenes! domestic ties, pecuniary interests, civic claims disintegrate the group. It is sad to think how possible such intercourse is in youth, and in youth only, as one sees it displayed in that fine and moving book *Trilby*, which does contrive to reflect the joy of the buoyant companionship of art. But the flush dies down, the insouciance departs, and with it the ardent generosity of life. Some day perhaps, when life has become simpler and wealth more equalised, when work is more distributed, when there is less production of unnecessary things, these groups will form themselves, and the frank, eager, vivid spirit of youth will last on into middle-age, and even into age itself. I do not think that this is wholly a dream; but we must first get rid of much of the pompous nonsense about money and position, which now spoils so many lives; and if we could be more genuinely interested in the beauty and complex charm and joy of life, we should think less and less of material things, be content with shelter, warmth, and food, and grudge the time we waste in providing things for which we have no real use, simply in order that, like the rich fool, we may congratulate ourselves on having much goods laid up for many years, when the end was hard at hand!

XII
MEMORY

Memory is for many people the only form of poetry which they indulge. If a soul turns to the future for consolation in a sad or wearied or disappointed present, it is in religion that hope and strength are sometimes found; but if it is a retrospective nature — and the poetical nature is generally retrospective, because poetry is concerned with the beauty of actual experience and actual things, rather than with the possible and the unknown — then it finds its medicine for the dreariness of life in memory. Of course there are many simple and healthy natures which do not concern themselves with visions at all — the little businesses, the daily pleasures, are quietly and even eagerly enjoyed. But the poetical nature is the nature that is not easily contented, because it tends to idealisation, to the thought that the present might easily be so much happier, brighter, more beautiful, than it is.

> *An eager soul that looks beyond*
> *And shivers in the midst of bliss,*
> *That cries, "I should not need despond,*
> *If this were otherwise, and this!"*

And so the soul that has seen much and enjoyed much and endured much, and whose whole life has been not spoiled, of course, but a little shadowed by the thought that the elements of happiness have never been quite as pure as it would have wished, turns back in thought to the old scenes of love and companionship, and evokes from the dark, as from the pages of some volume of photographs and records, the pictures of the past, retouching them, it is true, and adapting them, by deftly removing all the broken lights and intrusive anxieties, not into what they actually were, but into what they might have been. Carlyle laid his finger upon the truth of this power, when he said that the reason why the pictures of the past were always so golden in tone, so delicate in outline, was because the quality of fear was taken from them. It is the fear of what may be and what must be that overshadows present happiness; and if fear is taken from us we are happy. The strange thing is that we cannot learn not to be afraid, even though all the darkest and saddest of our experiences have left us unscathed; and if we could but find a reason for the mingling of fear with our lives, we should have gone far towards solving the riddle of the world.

This indulgence of memory is not necessarily a weakening or an enervating thing, so long as it does not come to us too early, or disengage us from needful activities. It is often not accompanied by any shadow of loss or bitterness. I remember once sitting with my beloved old nurse, when she was near her ninetieth year, in her little room, in which was gathered much of the old nursery furniture, the tiny chairs of the children, the store-cupboard with the farmyard pictures on the panel, the stuffed pet-birds — all the homely wrack of life; and we had been recalling many of the old childish incidents with laughter and smiles. When I rose to go, she sate still for a minute, and her eyes filled with quiet tears, "Ah, those were happy days!" she said. But there was no repining about it, no sense that it was better to forget old joys — rather a quiet pleasure that so much that was beautiful and tender was laid away in memory, and could neither be altered nor taken away. And one does not find in old people, whose memory of the past is clear, while their recollection of the present grows dim, any sense of pathos, but rather of pride and eagerness about recalling the minutest details of the vanished days. To feel the pathos of the past, as Tennyson expressed it in that wonderful and moving lyric, *Tears, idle tears*, is much more characteristic of youth. There is rather in serene old age a sense of pleasant triumph at having safely weathered the storms of fate, and left the tragedies of life behind. The aged would not as a rule live life over again, if they could. They are not disappointed in life. They have had, on the whole, what they hoped and desired. As Goethe said, in that deep and large maxim, "Of that which a man desires in his youth, he shall have enough in his age." That is one of the most singular things in life — at least this is my experience — how the things which one really desired, not the things which one ought to have desired, are showered upon one. I have been amazed and even stupefied sometimes to consider how my own little petty, foolish, whimsical desires have been faithfully and literally granted me. We most of us do really translate into fact what we desire, and as a rule we only fail to get the things which we have not desired enough. It is true indeed that we often find that what we desired was not worth getting; and we ought to be more afraid of our desires, not because we shall not get them, but because we shall almost certainly have them fulfilled. For myself I can only think with shame how closely my present conditions do resemble my young desires, in all their petty range, their trivial particularity. I suppose I have unconsciously pursued them, chosen them, grasped at them; and the shame of it is that if I had desired better things, I should assuredly have been given them. I see, or seem to see, the same thing in the lives of many that I know. What a man sows he shall reap! That is taken generally to mean that if he sows pleasure, he shall reap disaster; but it has a much truer and more terrible meaning than that — namely, that if a man sows the seed of small, trivial, foolish joys, the grain that he reaps is small, trivial, and foolish too. God is indeed in many ways an indulgent Father, like the Father in the parable of the Prodigal Son; and the best rebuke that He gives, if we have the wisdom to see it, is that He so often does hand us, with a smile, the very thing we have desired. And thus it is well to pray that He should put into our minds good desires, and that we should use our wills to keep ourselves from dwelling too much upon small and pitiful desires, for the fear is that they will be abundantly gratified.

And thus when the time comes for recollection, it is a very wonderful thing to look back over life, and see how eagerly gracious God has been to us. He knows very well that we cannot learn the paltry value of the things we desire, if they are withheld from us, but only if they are granted to us; and thus we have no reason to doubt His fatherly intention, because He does so much dispose life to please us. And we need not take it for granted that He will lead us by harsh and provocative discipline, though when He grants our desire, He sometimes sends leanness withal into our soul. Yet one of the things that strikes one most forcibly, as one grows older and learns something of the secrets of other lives, is how lightly and serenely men and women do often bear what might seem to be intolerable calamities. How universal an experience it is to find that when the expected calamity does come, it is an easier affair than we thought it, so that we say under the blow, "Is that really all?" In that wonderful book, the Diary of Sir Walter Scott, when his bankruptcy fell upon him, and all the schemes and designs that he had been carrying out, with the joyful zest of a child — his toy-castle, his feudal circle, his wide estate — were suddenly suspended, he wrote with an almost amused surprise that he found how little he really cared, and that the people who spoke tenderly and sympathetically to him, as though he must be reeling under the catastrophe, would themselves be amazed to find that he found himself as cheerful and undaunted as ever. Life is apt, for all vivid people, to be a species of high-hearted game: it is such fun to play it as eagerly as one can, and to persuade oneself that one really cares about the applause, the money, the fine house, the comforts, the deference, the convenience of it all. And yet, if there is anything noble in a man or woman, when the game is suddenly interrupted and the toys swept aside, they find that there is something exciting and stimulating in having to do without, in adapting themselves with zest to the new conditions. It was a good game enough, but the new game is better! The failure is to take it all heavily and seriously, to be solemn about it; for then failure is disconcerting indeed. But if one is interested in experience, but yet has the vitality to see how detached one really is from material things, how little they really affect us, then the change is almost grateful. It is the spirit of the game, the activity, the energy, that delights us, not the particular toy. And so the looking back on life ought never to be a mournful thing; it ought to be light-hearted, high-spirited, amusing. The spirit survives, and there is yet much experience ahead of us. We waste our sense of pathos very strangely over inanimate things. We get to feel about the things that surround us, our houses, our very chairs and tables, as if they were somehow things that were actually attached to us. We feel, when the old house that has belonged to our family passes into other hands, as though the rooms resented the intruders; as though our sofas and cabinets could not be at ease in other hands, as if they would almost prefer shabby and dusty inaction in our own lumber-room, to cheerful use in some other circle. This is a delusion of which we must make haste to get rid. It is the weakest sort of sentiment, and yet it is treasured by many natures as if it were something refined and noble. To yield to it, is to fetter our life with self-imposed and fantastic chains. There is no sort of reason why we should not love to live among familiar things; but to break our hearts over the loss of them is a real debasing of ourselves. We must learn to use the things of life very lightly and detachedly; and to entrench ourselves in trivial associations is simply to court dreariness and to fall into a stupor of the spirit.

And thus even our old memories must be treated with the same lightness and unaffectedness. We must do all we can to forget grief and disaster. We must not consecrate a shrine to sorrow and make the votive altar, as Dido did, into a *causa doloris*, an excuse for lamentation. We must not think it an honourable and chivalrous and noble thing to spend our time in broken-hearted solemnity in the vaults of perished joys. Or if we do it, we must frankly confess it to be a weakness and a languor of spirit, not believe it to be a thing which others ought to admire and respect. It was one of the base sentimentalities of the last century, a real sign of the decadence of life, that people felt it to be a fine thing to cherish grief, and to live resolutely with sighs and tears. The helpless widow of nineteenth-century fiction, shrouded in crape, and bursting into tears at the smallest sign of gaiety, was a wholly unlovely, affected, dramatic affair. And one of the surest signs of our present vitality is that this attitude has become not only unusual, but frankly absurd and unfashionable. There is an intense and gallant pathos about a nature broken by sorrow, making desperate attempts to be cheerful and active, and not to cast a shadow of grief upon others. There is no pathos at all in the sight of a person bent on emphasising his or her grief, on using it to make others uncomfortable, on extracting a recognition of its loyalty and fidelity and emotional fervour.

Of course there are some memories and experiences that must grave a deep and terrible mark upon the heart, the shock of which has been so severe, that the current of life must necessarily be altered by them. But even then it is better as far as possible to forget them and to put them away from us — at all events, not to indulge them or dwell in them. To yield is simply to delay the pilgrimage, to fall exhausted in some unhappy arbour by the road. The road has to be travelled, every inch of it, and it is better to struggle on in feebleness than to collapse in despair.

Mrs. Charles Kingsley, in her widowhood, once said to a friend, "Whenever I find myself thinking too much about Charles, I simply force myself to read the most exciting novel I can. He is there, he is waiting for me; and hearts were made to love with, not to break."

And as the years go on, even the most terrible memories grow to have the grace and beauty which nature lavishes on all the relics of extinct forces and spent agonies. They become like the old grey broken castle, with the grasses on its ledges, and the crows nesting in its parapets, rising blind and dumb on its green mound, with the hamlet at its feet; or like the craggy islet, severed by the raging sea from the towering headland, where the samphire sprouts in the rift, and the sea-birds roost, at whose foot the surges lap, and over whose head the landward wind blows swiftly all the day.

XIII
RETROSPECT

But one must not forget that after all memory has another side, too often a rueful side, and that it often seems to turn sour and poisonous in the sharp decline of fading life; and this ought not to be. I would like to describe a little experience of my own which came to me as a surprise, but showed me clearly enough what memory can be and what it rightly is, if it is to feed the spirit at all.

Not very long ago I visited Lincoln, where my father was Canon and Chancellor from 1872 to 1877. I had only been there once since then, and that was twenty-four years ago. When we lived there I was a small Eton boy, so that it was always holiday time there, and a place which recalls nothing but school holidays has perhaps an unfair advantage. Moreover it was a period quite unaccompanied, in our family life, by any sort of trouble, illness, or calamity. The Chancery of Lincoln is connected in my mind with no tragic or even sorrowful event whatever, and suggests no painful reminiscence. How many people, I wonder, can say that of any home that has sheltered them for so long?

Of course Lincoln itself, quite apart from any memories or associations, is a place to kindle much emotion. It was a fine sunny day there, and the colour of the whole place was amazing — the rich warm hue of the stone of which the Minster is built, which takes on a fine ochre-brown tinge where it is weathered, gives it a look of homely comfort, apart from the matchless dignity of clustered transept and soaring towers. Then the glowing and mellow brick of Lincoln, its scarlet roof tiles — what could be more satisfying for instance than the dash of vivid red in the tiling of the old Palace as you see it on the slope among its gardens from the opposite upland? — its smoke-blackened façades, the abundance, all over the hill, of old embowered gardens, full of trees and thickets and greenery, its grassy spaces, its creeper-clad houses; the whole effect is one of extraordinary richness of hue, of age vividly exuberant, splendidly adorned.

I wandered transported about Cathedral and close, and became aware then of how strangely unadventurous in the matter of exploration one had always been as a boy. It was true that we children had scampered with my father's master-key from end to end of the Cathedral — wet mornings used constantly to be spent there — so that I know every staircase, gallery, clerestory, parapet, triforium, and roof-vault of the building — but I found in the close itself many houses, alleys, little streets, which I had actually never seen, or even suspected their existence.

It was all full of little ghosts, and a tiny vignette shaped itself in memory at every corner, of some passing figure — a good-natured Canon, a youthful friend, Levite or Nethinim, or some deadly enemy, the son perhaps of some old-established denizen of the close, with whom for some unknown reason the Chancery school-room proclaimed an inflexible feud.

But when I came to see the old house itself — so little changed, so distinctly recollected — then I was indeed amazed at the torrent of little happy fragrant memories which seemed to pour from every doorway and window — the games, the meals, the plays, the literary projects, the readings, the telling of stories, the endless, pointless, enchanting wanderings with some breathless object in view, forgotten or transformed before it was ever attained or executed, of which children alone hold the secret.

Best of all do I recollect long summer afternoons spent in the great secluded high-walled garden at the back, with its orchard, its mound covered with thickets, and the old tower of the city wall, which made a noble fortress in games of prowess or adventure. I can see the figure of my father in his cassock, holding a little book, walking up and down among the gooseberry-beds half the morning, as he developed one of his unwritten sermons for the Minster on the following day.

I do not remember that very affectionate relations existed between us children; it was a society, based on good-humoured tolerance and a certain democratic respect for liberty, that nursery group; it had its cliques, its sections, its political emphasis, its diplomacies; but it was cordial rather than emotional, and bound together by common interests rather than by mutual devotion.

This, for instance, was one of the ludicrous incidents which came back to me. There was an odd little mediæval room on the ground-floor, given up as a sort of study, in the school sense, to my elder brother and myself. My younger brother, aged almost eight, to show his power, I suppose, or to protest against some probably quite real grievance or tangible indignity, came there secretly one morning in our absence, took a shovelful of red-hot coals from the fire, laid them on the hearth-rug, and departed. The conflagration was discovered in time, the author of the crime detected, and even the most tolerant of supporters of nursery anarchy could find nothing to criticise or condemn in the punishment justly meted out to the offender.

But here was the extraordinary part of it all. I am myself somewhat afraid of emotional retrospect, which seems to me as a rule to have a peculiarly pungent and unbearable smart about it. I do not as a rule like revisiting places which I have loved and where I have been happy; it is simply incurring quite unnecessary pain, and quite fruitless pain, deliberately to unearth buried memories of happiness.

Now at Lincoln the other day I found, to my wonder and relief, that there was not the least touch of regret, no sense of sorrow or loss in the air. I did not want it all back again, nor would I have lived through it again, even if I could have done so. The thought of returning to it seemed puerile; it was charming, delightful, all full of golden prospects and sunny mornings, but an experience which had yielded up its sweetness as a summer cloud yields its cooling rain, and passes over. Yet it was all a perfectly true, real, and actual part of my life, something of which I could never lose hold and for which I could always be frankly grateful. Life has been by no means a scene of untroubled happiness since then; but there came to me that day, walking along the fragrant garden-paths, very clearly and distinctly, the knowledge that one would not wish one's life to have been untroubled! Halcyon calm, heedless innocence, childish joy, was not after all the point — pretty things enough, but only as a change and a relief, or perhaps rather as a prelude to more serious business! I was, as a boy, afraid of life, hated its noise and scent, suspected it of cruelty and coarseness, wanted to keep it at arm's length. I feel very differently about life now; it's a boisterous business enough, but does not molest one unduly; and a very little courage goes a long way in dealing with it!

True, on looking back, the evolution was dim and obscure; there seemed many blind alleys and passages, many unnecessary winds and turns in the road; but for all that the trend was clear enough, at all events, to show that there was some great and not unkindly conspiracy about me and my concerns, involving every one else's concerns as well, some good-humoured mystery, with a dash of shadow and sorrow across it perhaps, which would be soon cleared up; some secret withheld as from a child, the very withholder of which seems to struggle with good-tempered laughter, partly at one's dulness in not being able to guess, partly at the pleasure in store.

I think it is our impatience, our claim to have everything questionable made instantly and perfectly plain to us, which does the mischief — that, and the imagination which never can forecast any relief or surcease of pain, and pays no heed whatever to the astounding brevity, the unutterable rapidity of human life.

So, as I walked in the old garden, I simply rejoiced that I had a share in the place which could not be gainsaid; and that, even if the high towers themselves, with their melodious bells, should crumble into dust, I still had my dear memory of it all: the old life, the old voices, looks, embraces, came back in little glimpses; yet it was far away, long past, and I did not wish it back; the present seemed a perfectly natural and beautiful sequence, and that past life an old sweet chapter of some happy book, which needs no rewriting.

So I looked back in joy and tenderness — and even with a sort of compassion; the child whom I saw sauntering along the grass paths of the garden, shaking the globed rain out of the poppy's head, gathering the waxen apples from the orchard grass, he was myself in very truth — there was no doubting that; I hardly felt different. But I had gained something which he had not got, some opening of eye and heart; and he had yet to bear, to experience, to pass through, the days which I had done with, and which, in spite of their much sweetness, had yet a bitterness, as of a healing drug, underneath them, and which I did not wish to taste again. No, I desired no renewal of old things, only the power of interpreting the things that were new, and through which even now one was passing swiftly and carelessly, as the boy ran among the fruit-trees of the garden; but it was not the golden fragrant husk of happiness that one wanted, but the seed hidden within it — experience was made sweet just that one might be tempted to live! Yet the end of it all was not the pleasure or the joy that came and passed, the gaiety, even the innocence of childhood, but something stern and strong, which hardly showed at all at first, but at last seemed like the slow work of the graver of gems brushing away the glittering crystalline dust from the intaglio.

XIV
HUMOUR

The Castle of *Joyous Gard* was always full of laughter; not the wild giggling, I think, of reckless people, which the writer of Proverbs said was like the crackling of thorns under a pot; that is a wearisome and even an ugly thing, because it does not mean that people are honestly amused, but have some basely exciting thing in their minds. Laughter must be light-hearted, not light-minded. Still less was it the dismal tittering of ill-natured people over mean gossip, which is another of the ugly sounds of life. No, I think it was rather the laughter of cheerful people, glad to be amused, who hardly knew that they were laughing; that is a wholesome exercise enough. It was the laughter of men and women, with heavy enough business behind them and before them, but yet able in leisurely hours to find life full of merriment — the voice of joy and health! And I am sure too that it was not the guarded condescending laughter of saints who do not want to be out of sympathy with their neighbours, and laugh as precisely and punctually as they might respond to a liturgy, if they discover that they are meant to be amused!

Humour is one of the characteristics of *Joyous Gard*, not humour resolutely cultivated, but the humour which comes from a sane and healthy sense of proportion; and is a sign of light-heartedness rather than a thing aimed at; a thing which flows naturally into the easy spaces of life, because it finds the oddities of life, the peculiarities of people, the incongruities of thought and speech, both charming and delightful.

It is a great misfortune that so many people think it a mark of saintliness to be easily shocked, whereas the greatest saints of all are the people who are never shocked; they may be distressed, they may wish things different; but to be shocked is often nothing but a mark of vanity, a self-conscious desire that others should know how high one's standard, how sensitive one's conscience is. I do not of course mean that one is bound to join in laughter, however coarse a jest may be; but the best-bred and finest-tempered people steer past such moments with a delicate tact; contrive to show that an ugly jest is not so much a thing to be disapproved of and rebuked, as a sign that the jester is not recognising the rights of his company, and outstepping the laws of civility and decency.

It is a very difficult thing to say what humour is, and probably it is a thing that is not worth trying to define. It resides in the incongruity of speech and behaviour with the surrounding circumstances.

I remember once seeing two tramps disputing by the roadside, with the gravity which is given to human beings by being slightly overcome with drink. I suppose that one ought not to be amused by the effects of drunkenness, but after all one does not wish people to be drunk that one may be amused. The two tramps in question were ragged and infinitely disreputable. Just as I came up, the more tattered of the two flung his hat on the ground, with a lofty gesture like that of a king abdicating, and said, "I'll go no further with you!" The other said, "Why do you say that? Why will you go no further with me?" The first replied, "No, I'll go no further with you!" The other said, "I must know why you will go no further with me — you must tell me that!" The first replied, with great dignity, "Well, I will tell you that! It lowers my self-respect to be seen with a man like you!"

That is the sort of incongruity I mean. The tragic solemnity of a man who might have changed clothes with the nearest scarecrow without a perceptible difference, and whose life was evidently not ordered by any excessive self-respect, falling back on the dignity of human nature in order to be rid of a companion as disreputable as himself, is what makes the scene so grotesque, and yet in a sense so impressive, because it shows a lurking standard of conduct which no pitiableness of degradation could obliterate. I think that is a good illustration of what I mean by humour, because in the presence of such a scene it is possible to have three perfectly distinct emotions. One may be sorry with all one's heart that men should fall to such conditions, and feel that it is a stigma on our social machinery that it should be so. Those two melancholy figures were a sad blot upon the wholesome countryside! Yet one may also discern a hope in the mere possibility of framing an ideal under such discouraging circumstances, which will be, I have no sort of doubt, a seed of good in the upward progress of the poor soul which grasped it; because indeed I have no doubt that the miserable creature *is* on an upward path, and that even if there is no prospect for him in this life of anything but a dismal stumbling down into disease and want, yet I do not in the least believe that that is the end of his horizon or his pilgrimage; and thirdly, one may be genuinely and not in the least evilly amused at the contrast between the disreputable squalor of the scene and the lofty claim advanced. The three emotions are not at all inconsistent. The pessimistic moralist might say that it was all very shocking, the optimistic moralist might say that it was hopeful, the unreflective humourist might simply be transported by the absurdity; yet not to be amused at such a scene would appear to me to be both dull and priggish. It seems to me to be a false solemnity to be shocked at any lapses from perfection; a man might as well be shocked at the existence of a poisonous snake or a ravening tiger. One must "see life steadily and see it whole," and though we may and must hope that we shall struggle upwards out of the mess, we may still be amused at the dolorous figures we cut in the mire.

I was once in the company of a grave, decorous, and well-dressed person who fell helplessly into a stream off a stepping-stone. I had no wish that he should fall, and I was perfectly conscious of intense sympathy with his discomfort; but I found the scene quite inexpressibly diverting, and I still simmer with laughter at the recollection of the disappearance of the trim figure, and his furious emergence, like an oozy water-god, from the pool. It is not in the least an ill-natured laughter. I did not desire the catastrophe, and I would have prevented it if I could; but it was dreadfully funny for all that; and if a similar thing had happened to myself, I should not resent the enjoyment of the scene by a spectator, so long as I was helped and sympathised with, and the merriment decently repressed before me.

I think that what is called practical joking, which aims at deliberately producing such situations, is a wholly detestable thing. But it is one thing to sacrifice another person's comfort to one's laughter, and quite another to be amused at what a fire-insurance policy calls the act of God.

And I am very sure of this, that the sane, healthy, well-balanced nature must have a fund of wholesome laughter in him, and that so far from trying to repress a sense of humour, as an unkind, unworthy, inhuman thing, there is no capacity of human nature which makes life so frank and pleasant a business. There are no companions so delightful as the people for whom one treasures up jests and reminiscences, because one is sure that they will respond to them and enjoy them; and indeed I have found that the power of being irresponsibly amused has come to my aid in the middle of really tragic and awful circumstances, and has relieved the strain more than anything else could have done.

I do not say that humour is a thing to be endlessly indulged and sought after; but to be genuinely amused is a sign of courage and amiability, and a sign too that a man is not self-conscious and self-absorbed. It ought not to be a settled pre-occupation. Nothing is more wearisome than the habitual jester, because that signifies that a man is careless and unobservant of the moods of others. But it is a thing which should be generously and freely mingled with life; and the more sides that a man can see to any situation, the more rich and full his nature is sure to be.

After all, our power of taking a light-hearted view of life is proportional to our interest in it, our belief in it, our hopes of it. Of course, if we conclude from our little piece of remembered experience, that life is a woeful thing, we shall be apt to do as the old poets thought the nightingale did, to lean our breast against a thorn, that we may suffer the pain which we propose to utter in liquid notes. But that seems to me a false sentiment and an artificial mode of life, to luxuriate in sorrow; even that is better than being crushed by it; but we may be sure that if we wilfully allow ourselves to be one-sided, it is a delaying of our progress. All experience comes to us that we may not be one-sided; and if we learn to weep with those that weep, we must remember that it is no less our business to rejoice with those that rejoice. We are helped beyond measure by those who can tell us and convince us, as poets can, that there is something beautiful in sorrow and loss and severed ties; by those who show us the splendour of courage and patience and endurance; but the true faith is to believe that the end is joy; and we therefore owe perhaps the largest debt of all to those who encourage us to enjoy, to laugh, to smile, to be amused.

And so we must not retire into our fortress simply for lonely visions, sweet contemplation, gentle imagination; there are rooms in our castle fit for that, the little book-lined cell, facing the sunset, the high parlour, where the gay, brisk music comes tripping down from the minstrels' gallery, the dim chapel for prayer, and the chamber called *Peace* — where the pilgrim slept till break of day, "and then he awoke and sang"; but there is also the well-lighted hall, with cheerful company coming and going; where we must put our secluded, wistful, sorrowful thought aside, and mingle briskly with the pleasant throng, not steeling ourselves to mirth and movement, but simply glad and grateful to be there.

It was while I was writing these pages that a friend told me that he had recently met a man, a merchant, I think, who did me the honour to discuss my writings at a party and to pronounce an opinion upon them. He said that I wrote many things which I did not believe, and then stood aside, and was amused in a humorous mood to see that other people believed them. It would be absurd to be, or even to feel, indignant at such a travesty of my purpose as this, and indeed I think that one is never very indignant at misrepresentation unless one's mind accuses itself of its being true or partially true.

It is indeed true that I have said things about which I have since changed my mind, as indeed I hope I shall continue to change it, and as swiftly as possible, if I see that the former opinions are not justified. To be thus criticised is, I think, the perfectly natural penalty of having tried to be serious without being also solemn; there are many people, and many of them very worthy people, like our friend the merchant, who cannot believe one is in earnest if one is not also heavy-handed. Earnestness is mixed up in their minds with bawling and sweating; and indeed it is quite true that most people who are willing to bawl and sweat in public, feel earnestly about the subjects to which they thus address themselves. But I do not see that earnestness is in the least incompatible with lightness of touch and even with humour, though I have sometimes been accused of displaying none. Socrates was in earnest about his ideas, but the penalty he paid for treating them lightly was that he was put to death for being so sceptical. I should not at all like the idea of being put to death for my ideas; but I am wholly in earnest about them, and have never consciously said anything in which I did not believe.

But I will go one step further and say that I think that many earnest men do great harm to the causes they advocate, because they treat ideas so heavily, and divest them of their charm. One of the reasons why virtue and goodness are not more attractive is because they get into the hands of people without lightness or humour, and even without courtesy; and thus the pursuit of virtue seems not only to the young, but to many older people, to be a boring occupation, and to be conducted in an atmosphere heavy with disapproval, with dreariness and dulness and tiresomeness hemming the neophyte in, like fat bulls of Bashan. It is because I should like to rescue goodness, which is the best thing in the world, next to love, from these growing influences, that I have written as I have done; but there is no lurking cynicism in my books at all, and the worst thing I can accuse myself of is a sense of humour, perhaps whimsical and childish, which seems to me to make a pleasant and refreshing companion, as one passes on pilgrimage in search of what I believe to be very high and heavenly things indeed.

XV

VISIONS

I used as a child to pore over the Apocalypse, which I thought by far the most beautiful and absorbing of all the books of the Bible; it seemed full of rich and dim pictures, things which I could not interpret and did not wish to interpret, the shining of clear gemlike walls, lonely riders, amazing monsters, sealed books, all of which took perfectly definite shape in the childish imagination. The consequence is that I can no more criticise it than I could criticise old tapestries or pictures familiar from infancy. They are there, just so, and any difference of form is inconceivable.

In one point, however, the strange visions have come to hold for me an increased grandeur; I used to think of much of it as a sort of dramatic performance, self-consciously enacted for the benefit of the spectator; but now I think of it as an awful and spontaneous energy of spiritual life going on, of which the prophet was enabled to catch a glimpse. Those 'voices crying day and night' 'the new song that was sung before the throne,' the cry of "Come and see" — these were but part of a vast and urgent business, which the prophet was allowed to overhear. It is not a silent place, that highest heaven, of indolence and placid peace, but a scene of fierce activity and the clamour of mighty voices.

And it is the same too of another strange scene — the Transfiguration; not an impressive spectacle arranged for the apostles, but a peep into the awful background behind life. Let me use a simple parable: imagine a man who had a friend whom he greatly admired and loved, and suppose him to be talking with his friend, who suddenly excuses himself on the plea of an engagement and goes out; and the other follows him, out of curiosity, and sees him meet another man and talk intently with him, not deferentially or humbly, but as a man talks with an equal. And then drawing nearer he might suddenly see that the man his friend has gone out to meet, and with whom he is talking so intently, is some high minister of State, or even the King himself!

That is a simple comparison, to make clear what the apostles might have felt. They had gone into the mountain expecting to hear their Master speak quietly to them or betake himself to silent prayer; and then they find him robed in light and holding converse with the spirits of the air, telling his plans, so to speak, to two great prophets of the ancient world.

If this had been but a pageant enacted for their benefit to dazzle and bewilder them, it would have been a poor and self-conscious affair; but it becomes a scene of portentous mystery, if one thinks of them as being permitted to have a glimpse of the high, urgent, and terrifying things that were going on all the time in the unseen background of the Saviour's mind. The essence of the greatness of the scene is that it was *overheard.* And thus I think that wonder and beauty, those two mighty forces, take on a very different value for us when we can come to realise that they are small hints given us, tiny glimpses conceded to us, of some very great and mysterious thing that is pressingly and speedily proceeding, every day and every hour, in the vast background of life; and we ought to realise that it is not only human life as we see it which is the active, busy, forceful thing; that the world with all its noisy cities, its movements and its bustle, is not a burning point hung in darkness and silence, but that it is just a little fretful affair with infinitely larger, louder, fiercer, stronger powers, working, moving, pressing onwards, thundering in the background; and that the huge forces, laws, activities, behind the world, are not perceived by us any more than we perceive the vast motion of great winds, except in so far as we see the face of the waters rippled by them, or the trees bowed all one way in their passage.

It is very easy to be so taken up with the little absorbing businesses, the froth and ripple of life, that we forget what great and secret influences they must be that cause them; we must not forget that we are only like children playing in the nursery of a palace, while in the Council-room beneath us a debate may be going on which is to affect the lives and happiness of thousands of households.

And therefore the more that we make up our little beliefs and ideas, as a man folds up a little packet of food which he is to eat on a journey, and think in so doing that we have got a satisfactory explanation of all our aims and problems, the more utterly we are failing to take in the significance of what is happening. We must never allow ourselves to make up our minds, and to get our theories comfortably settled, because then experience is at an end for us, and we shall see no more than we expect to see. We ought rather to be amazed and astonished, day by day, at all the wonderful and beautiful things we encounter, the marvellous hints of loveliness which we see in faces, woods, hills, gardens, all showing some tremendous force at work, often thwarted, often spoiled, but still working, with an infinity of tender patience, to make the world exquisite and fine. There are ugly, coarse, disgusting things at work too — we cannot help seeing that; but even many of them seem to be destroying, in corruption and evil odour, something that ought not to be there, and striving to be clean and pure again.

I often wonder whose was the mind that conceived the visions of the Apocalypse; if we can trust tradition, it was a confined and exiled Christian in a lonely island, whose spirit reached out beyond the little crags and the beating seas of his prison, and in the seeming silent heaven detected the gathering of monsters, the war of relentless forces — and beyond it all the radiant energies of saints, glad to be together and unanimous, in a place where light and beauty at last could reign triumphant.

I know no literature more ineffably dreary than the parcelling out of these wild and glorious visions, the attaching of them to this and that petty human fulfilment. That is not the secret of the Apocalypse! It is rather as a painter may draw a picture of two lovers sitting together at evening in a latticed chamber, holding each other's hands, gazing in each other's eyes. He is not thinking of particular persons in an actual house; it is rather a hint of love making itself manifest, recognising itself to be met with an answering rapture. And what I think that the prophet meant was rather to show that we must not be deceived by cares and anxieties and daily business; but that behind the little simmering of the world was a tumult of vast forces, voices crying and answering, thunder, fire, infinite music. It is all a command to recognise unseen greatness, to take every least experience we can, and crush from it all its savour; not to be afraid of the great emotions of the world, love and sorrow and loss; but only to be afraid of what is petty and sordid and mean. And then perhaps, as in that other vision, we may ascend once into a mountain, and there in weariness and drowsiness, dumbly bewildered by the night and the cold and the discomforts of the unkindly air, life may be for a moment transfigured into a radiant figure, still familiar though so glorified; and we may see it for once touch hands and exchange words with old and wise spirits; and all this not only to excite us and bewilder us, but so that by the drawing of the veil aside, we may see for a moment that there is some high and splendid secret, some celestial business proceeding with solemn patience and strange momentousness, a rite which if we cannot share, we may at least know is there, and waiting for us, the moment that we are strong enough to take our part!

XVI
THOUGHT

A friend of mine had once a strange dream; he seemed to himself to be walking in a day of high summer on a grassy moorland leading up to some fantastically piled granite crags. He made his way slowly thither; it was terribly hot there among the sun-warmed rocks, and he found a little natural cave, among the great boulders, fringed with fern. There he sate for a long time while the sun passed over, and a little breeze came wandering up the moor. Opposite him as he sate was the face of a great pile of rocks, and while his eye dwelt upon it it suddenly began to wink and glisten with little moving points, dots so minute that he could hardly distinguish them. Suddenly, as if at a signal, the little points dropped from the rock, and the whole surface seemed alive with gossamer threads, as if a silken, silvery curtain had been let down; presently the little dots reached the grass and began to crawl over it; and then he saw that each of them was attached to one of the fine threads; and he thought that they were a colony of minute spiders, living on the face of the rocks. He got up to see this wonder close at hand, but the moment he moved, the whole curtain was drawn up with incredible swiftness, as if the threads were highly elastic; and when he reached the rock, it was as hard and solid as before, nor could he discover any sign of the little creatures. "Ah," he said to himself in the dream, "that is the meaning of the *living* rock!" and he became aware, he thought, that all rocks and stones on the surface of the earth must be thus endowed with life, and that the rocks were, so to speak, but the shell that contained these innumerable little creatures, incredibly minute, living, silken threads, with a small head, like boring worms, inhabiting burrows which went far into the heart of the granite, and each with a strong retractile power.

I told this dream to a geologist the other day, who laughed, "An ingenious idea," he said, "and there may even be something in it! It is not by any means certain that stones do not have a certain obscure life of their own; I have sometimes thought that their marvellous cohesion may be a sign of life, and that if life were withdrawn, a mountain might in a moment become a heap of sliding sand."

My friend said that the dream made such an impression upon him that for a time he found it hard to believe that stones and rocks had not this strange and secret life lurking in their recesses; and indeed it has since stood to me as a symbol of life, haunting and penetrating all the very hardest and driest things. It seems to me that just as there are almost certainly more colours than our eyes can perceive, and sounds either too acute or too deliberate for our ears to hear, so the domain of life may be much further extended in the earth, the air, the waters, than we can tangibly detect.

It seems too to show me that it is our business to try ceaselessly to discover the secret life of thought in the world; not to conclude that there is no vitality in thought unless we can ourselves at once perceive it. This is particularly the case with books. Sometimes, in our College Library, I take down an old folio from the shelves, and as I turn the crackling, stained, irregular pages — it may be a volume of controversial divinity or outworn philosophy — it seems impossible to imagine that it can ever have been woven out of the live brain of man, or that any one can ever have been found to follow those old, vehement, insecure arguments, starting from unproved data, and leading to erroneous and fanciful conclusions. The whole thing seems so faded, so dreary, so remote from reality, that one cannot even dimly imagine the frame of mind which originated it, and still less the mood which fed upon such things.

Yet I very much doubt if the aims, ideas, hopes of man, have altered very much since the time of the earliest records. When one comes to realise that geologists reckon a period of thirty million years at least, while the Triassic rocks, that is the lowest stratum that shows signs of life, were being laid down; and that all recorded history is but an infinitesimal drop in the ocean of unrecorded time, one sees at least that the force behind the world, by whatever name we call it, is a force that cannot by any means be hurried, but that it works with a leisureliness which we with our brief and hasty span of life cannot really in any sense conceive. Still it seems to have a plan! Those strange horned, humped, armoured beasts of prehistoric rocks are all bewilderingly like ourselves so far as physical construction goes; they had heart, brain, eyes, lungs, legs, a similarly planned skeleton; it seems as if the creative spirit was working by a well-conceived pattern, was trying to make a very definite kind of thing; there is not by any means an infinite variety, when one considers the sort of creatures that even a man could devise and invent, if he tried.

There is the same sort of continuity and unity in thought The preoccupations of man are the same in all ages — to provide for his material needs, and to speculate what can possibly happen to his spirit, when the body, broken by accident or disease or decay, can no longer contain his soul. The best thought of man has always been centred on trying to devise some sort of future hope which could encourage him to live eagerly, to endure patiently, to act rightly. As science opens her vast volume before us, we naturally become more and more impatient of the hasty guesses of man, in religion and philosophy, to define what we cannot yet know; but we ought to be very tender of the old passionate beliefs, the intense desire to credit noble and lofty spirits, such as Buddha and Mahomet, with some source of divinely given knowledge. Yet of course there is an inevitable sadness when we find the old certainties dissolving in mist; and we must be very careful to substitute for them, if they slip from our grasp, some sort of principle which will give us freshness and courage. To me, I confess, the tiny certainties of science are far more inspiring than the most ardent reveries of imaginative men. The knowledge that there is in the world an inflexible order, and that we shall see what we shall see, and not what we would like to believe, is infinitely refreshing and sustaining. I feel that I am journeying onwards into what is unknown to me, but into something which is inevitably there, and not to be altered by my own hopes and fancies. It is like taking a voyage, the pleasure of which is that the sights in store are unexpected and novel; for a voyage would be a very poor thing if we knew exactly what lay ahead, and poorer still if we could determine beforehand what we meant to see, and could only behold the pictures of our own imaginations. That is the charm and the use of experience, that it is not at all what we expect or hope. It is in some ways sadder and darker; but it is in most ways far more rich and wonderful and radiant than we had dreamed.

What I grow impatient of are the censures of rigid people, who desire to limit the hopes and possibilities of others by the little foot-rule which they have made for themselves. That is a very petty and even a very wicked thing to do, that old persecuting instinct which says, "I will make it as unpleasant for you as I can, if you will not consent at all events to pretend to believe what I think it right to believe." A man of science does not want to persecute a child who says petulantly that he will not believe the law of gravity. He merely smiles and goes on his way. The law of gravity can look after itself! Persecution is as often as not an attempt to reassure oneself about one's own beliefs; it is not a sign of an untroubled faith.

We must not allow ourselves to be shaken by any attempt to dictate to us what we should believe. We need not always protest against it, unless we feel it a duty to do so; we may simply regard another's certainties as things which are not and cannot be proved. Argument on such subjects is merely a waste of time; but at the same time we ought to recognise the vitality which lies behind such tenacious beliefs, and be glad that it is there, even if we think it to be mistaken.

And this brings me back to my first point, which is that it is good for us to try to realise the hidden life of the world, and to rejoice in it even though it has no truth for us. We must never disbelieve in life, even though in sickness and sorrow and age it may seem to ebb from us; and we must try at all costs to recognise it, to sympathise with it, to put ourselves in touch with it, even though it takes forms unintelligible and even repugnant to ourselves.

Let me try to translate this into very practical matters. We many of us find ourselves in a fixed relation to a certain circle of people. We cannot break with them or abandon them. Perhaps our livelihood depends upon them, or theirs upon us. Yet we may find them harsh, unsympathetic, unkind, objectionable. What are we to do? Many people let the whole tangle go, and just creep along, doing what they do not like, feeling unappreciated and misunderstood, just hoping to avoid active collisions and unpleasant scenes. That is a very spiritless business! What we ought to do is to find points of contact, even at the cost of some repression of our own views and aims. And we ought too to nourish a fine life of our own, to look into the lives of other people, which can be done perhaps best in large books, fine biographies, great works of imagination and fiction. We must not drowse and brood in our own sombre corner, when life is flowing free and full outside, as in some flashing river. However little chance we may seem to have of *doing* anything, we can at least determine to *be* something; not to let our life be filled, like some base vessel, with the offscourings and rinsings of other spirits, but to remember that the water of life is given freely to all who come. That is the worst of our dull view of the great Gospel of Christ. We think — I do not say this profanely but seriously — of that water of life as a series of propositions like the Athanasian Creed!

Christ meant something very different by the water of life. He meant that the soul that was athirst could receive a draught of a spring of cool refreshment and living joy. He did not mean a set of doctrines; doctrines are to life what parchments and title-deeds are to an estate with woods and waters, fields and gardens, houses and cottages, and live people moving to and fro. It is of no use to possess the title-deed if one does not visit one's estate. Doctrines are an attempt to state, in bare and precise language, ideas and thoughts dear and fresh to the heart. It is in qualities, hopes, and affections that we live; and if our eyes are opened, we can see, as my friend dreamed he saw, the surface of the hard rock full of moving points, and shimmering with threads of swift life, when the sun has fallen from the height, and the wind comes cool across the moor from the open gates of the evening.

XVII
ACCESSIBILITY

I was greatly interested the other day by seeing a photograph, in his old age, of Henry Phillpotts, the redoubtable Bishop of Exeter, who lost more money in lawsuits with clergymen than any Bishop, I suppose, who ever lived. He sate, the old man, in his clumsily fitting gaiters, bowed or crouched in an armchair, reading a letter. His face was turned to the spectator; with his stiff, upstanding hair, his outthrust lip, his corrugated brow, and the deep pouched lines beneath his eyes, he looked like a terrible old lion, who could no longer spring, but who had not forgotten how to roar. His face was full of displeasure and anger. I remembered that a clergyman once told me how he had been sitting next the Bishop at a dinner of parsons, and a young curate, sitting on the other side of the Bishop, affronted him by believing him to be deaf, and by speaking very loudly and distinctly to him. The Bishop at last turned to him, with a furious visage, and said, "I would have you to understand, sir, that I am not deaf!" This disconcerted the young man so much that he could neither speak nor eat. The old Bishop turned to my friend, and said, in a heavy tone, "I'm not fit for society!" Indeed he was not, if he could unchain so fierce a beast on such slight provocation.

And there are many other stories of the bitter things he said, and how his displeasure could brood like a cloud over a whole company. He was a gallant old figure, it is true, very energetic, very able, determined to do what he thought right, and infinitely courageous. I mused over the portrait, thought how lifelike and picturesque it was, and how utterly unlike one's idea of an aged Christian or a chief shepherd. In his beautiful villa by the sea, with its hanging woods and gardens, ruling with diligence, he seemed to me more like a stoical Roman Emperor, or a tempestuous Sadducee, the spirit of the world incarnate. One wondered what it could have been that had drawn him to Christ, or what part he would have taken if he had been on the Sanhedrin that judged Him!

It seems to me that one of the first characteristics which one ought to do one's best to cast out of one's life is that of formidableness. Yet to tell a man that he is formidable is not an accusation that is often resented. He may indulgently deprecate it, but it seems to most people a sort of testimonial to their force and weight and influence, a penalty that they have to pay for being effective, a matter of prestige and honour. Of course, an old, famous, dignified man who has played a great part on the stage of life must necessarily be approached by the young with a certain awe. But there is no charm in the world more beautiful than the charm which can permeate dignity, give confidence, awake affection, dissipate dread. But if a man of that sort indulges his moods, says what he thinks bluntly and fiercely, has no mercy on feebleness or ignorance, he can be a very dreadful personage indeed!

Accessibility is one of the first of Christian virtues; but it is not always easy to practise, because a man of force and ability, who is modest and shy, forgets as life goes on how much more his influence is felt. He himself does not feel at all different from what he was when he was young, when he was snubbed and silenced and set down in argument. Perhaps he feels that the world is a kinder and an easier place, as he grows into deference and esteem, but it is the surest sign of a noble and beautiful character if the greater he becomes the more simple and tender he also becomes.

I was greatly interested the other day in attending a meeting at which, among other speakers, two well-known men spoke. The first was a man of great renown and prestige, and he made a very beautiful, lofty, and tender discourse; but, from some shyness or gravity of nature, he never smiled nor looked at his audience; and thus, fine though his speech was, he never got into touch with us at all. The second speech was far more obvious and commonplace, but the speaker, on beginning, cast a friendly look round and smiled on the audience; and he did the same all the time, so that one had at once a friendly sense of contact and geniality, and I felt that every word was addressed to me personally. That is what it is to be accessible!

One of the best ways in which we can keep the spirit of poetry — by which I mean the higher, sweeter, purer influences of thought — alive in one's heart, is by accessibility — by determining to speak freely of what one admires and loves, what moves and touches one, what keeps one's mind upon the inner and finer life. It is not always possible or indeed convenient for younger people to do this, for reasons which are not wholly bad reasons. Young people ought not to be too eager to take the lead in talk, nor ought they to be too openly impatient of the more sedate and prosaic discourse of their elders; and then, too, there is a time for all things; one cannot keep the mind always on the strain; and the best and most beautiful things are apt to come in glimpses and hints, and are not always arrived at by discussion and argument.

There is a story of a great artist full of sympathy and kindness, to whom in a single day three several people came to confide sad troubles and trials. The artist told the story to his wife in the evening. He said that he was afraid that the third of the visitors thought him strangely indifferent and even unkind. "The fact was," he said, "that my capacity for sympathy was really exhausted. I had suffered so much from the first two recitals that I could not be sorry any more. I *said* I was sorry, and I *was* sorry far down in my mind, but I could not *feel* sorry. I had given all the sympathy I had, and it was no use going again to the well when there was no more water." This shows that one cannot command emotion, and that one must not force even thoughts of beauty upon others. We must bide our time, we must adapt ourselves, and we must not be instant in season and out of season. Yet neither must we be wholly at the mercy of moods. In religion, the theory of liturgical worship is an attempt to realise that we ought to practise religious emotion with regularity. We do not always feel we are miserable sinners when we say so, and we sometimes feel that we are when we do not say it; but it is better to confess what we know to be true, even if at that moment we do not feel it to be true.

We ought not then always, out of modesty, to abstain from talking about the things for which we care. A foolish shyness will sometimes keep two sympathetic people from ever talking freely together of their real hopes and interests. We are terribly afraid in England of what we call priggishness. It is on the whole a wholesome tendency, but it is the result of a lack of flexibility of mind. What we ought to be afraid of is not seriousness and earnestness, but of solemnity and pomposity. We ought to be ready to vary our mood swiftly, and even to see the humorous side of sacred and beautiful things. The oppressiveness of people who hold a great many things sacred, and cannot bear that they should be jested about, is very great. There is nothing that takes all naturalness out of intercourse more quickly than the habit which some people have of begging that a subject may not be pursued "because it is one on which I feel very deeply." That is the essence of priggishness, to feel that our reasons are better, our motives purer, than the reasons of other people, and that we have the privilege of setting a standard. Conscious superiority is the note of the prig; and we have the right to dread it.

But the Gospel again is full of precepts in favour of frankness, outspokenness, letting light shine out, speaking sincerely; only it must not be done provokingly, condescendingly, solemnly. It is well for every one to have a friend or friends with whom he can talk quite unaffectedly about what he cares for and values; and he ought to be able to say to such a friend, "I cannot talk about these things now; I am in a dusty, prosaic, grubby mood, and I want to make mudpies"; the point is to be natural, and yet to keep a watch upon nature; not to force her into cramped postures, and yet not to indulge her in rude, careless, and vulgar postures. It is a bad sign in friendship, if intimacy seems to a man to give him the right to be rude, coarse, boisterous, censorious, if he will. He may sometimes be betrayed into each and all of these things, and be glad of a safety-valve for his ill-humours, knowing that he will not be permanently misunderstood by a sympathetic friend. But there must be a discipline in all these things, and nature must often give way and be broken in; frankness must not degenerate into boorishness, and liberty must not be the power of interfering with the liberty of the friend. One must force oneself to be courteous, interested, sweet-tempered, when one feels just the contrary; one must keep in sight the principle, and if violence must be done, it must not be done to the better nature. Least of all must one deliberately take up the rôle of exercising influence. That is a sad snare to many fine natures. One sees a weak, attractive character, and it seems so tempting to train it up a stick, to fortify it, to mould it. If one is a professed teacher, one has to try this sometimes; but even then, the temptation to drive rather than lead must be strenuously resisted.

I have always a very dark suspicion of people who talk of spheres of influence, and who enjoy consciously affecting other lives. If this is done professionally, as a joyful sort of exercise, it is deadly. The only excuse for it is that one really cares for people and longs to be of use; one cannot pump one's own tastes and character into others. The only hope is that they should develop their own qualities. Other people ought not to be 'problems' to us; they may be mysteries, but that is quite another thing. To love people, if one can, is the only way. To find out what is lovable in them and not to try to discover what is malleable in them is the secret. A wise and witty lady, who knows that she is tempted to try to direct other lives, told me that one of her friends once remonstrated with her by saying that she ought to leave something for God to do!

I know a very terrible and well-meaning person, who once spoke severely to me for treating a matter with levity. I lost my temper, and said, "You may make me ashamed of it, if you can, but you shall not bully me into treating a matter seriously which I think is wholly absurd." He said, "You do not enough consider the grave issues which may be involved." I replied that to be for ever considering graver issues seemed to me to make life stuffy and unwholesome. My censor sighed and shook his head.

We cannot coerce any one into anything good. We may salve our own conscience by trying to do so, we may even level an immediate difficulty; but a free and generous desire to be different is the only hope of vital change. The detestable Puritan fibre that exists in many of us, which is the most utterly unchristian thing I know, tempts us to feel that no discipline is worth anything unless it is dark and gloomy; but that is the discipline of the law-court and the prison, and has never remedied anything since the world began. Wickedness is nearly always, perhaps always, a moral invalidism, and we shall see some day that to punish men for crime by being cruel to them is like condemning a man to the treadmill for having typhoid fever. I can only say that the more I have known of human beings, and the older I grow, the more lovable, gentle, sweet-tempered I have found them to be.

The life of Carlyle seems to me to be one of the most terrible and convincing documents in the world in proof of what I have been saying. The old man was so bent on battering and bumping people into righteousness, so in love with spluttering and vituperating and thundering all over the place, that he missed the truest and sweetest ministry of love. He broke his wife's heart, and it is idle to pretend he did not. Mrs. Carlyle was a sharp-edged woman too, and hurt her own life by her bitter trenchancy. But there was enough true love and loyalty and chivalry in the pair to furnish out a hundred marriages. Yet one sees Carlyle stamping and cursing through life, and never seeing what lay close to his hand. I admire his life not because it was a triumph, but because it was such a colossal failure, and so finely atoned for by the noble and great-minded repentance of a man who recognised at last that it was of no use to begin by trying to be ruler over ten cities, unless he was first faithful in a few things.

XVIII
SYMPATHY

But there is one thing which we must constantly bear in mind, and which all enthusiastic people must particularly recollect, namely, that our delight and interest in life must be large, tolerant, and sympathetic, and that we must not only admit but welcome an immense variety of interest. We must above all things be just, and we must be ready to be both interested and amused by people whom we do not like. The point is that minds should be fresh and clear, rather than stagnant and lustreless. Enthusiastic people, who feel very strongly and eagerly the beauty of one particular kind of delight, are sadly apt to wish to impose their own preferences upon other minds, and not to believe in the worth of others' preferences. Thus the men who feel very ardently the beauty of the Greek Classics are apt to insist that all boys shall be brought up upon them; and the same thing happens in other matters. We must not make a moral law out of our own tastes and preferences, and we must be content that others should feel the appeal of other sorts of beauty; that was the mistake which dogged the radiant path of Ruskin from first to last, that he could not bear that other people should have their own preferences, but considered that any dissidence from his own standards was of the nature of sin. If we insist on all agreeing with ourselves it is sterile enough; but if we begin to call other people hard names, and suspecting or vituperating their motives for disagreeing with us, we sin both against Love and Light. It was that spirit which called forth from Christ the sternest denunciation which ever fell from his lips. The Pharisees tried to discredit His work by representing Him as in league with the powers of evil; and this sin, which is the imputing of evil motives to actions and beliefs that appear to be good, because our own beliefs are too narrow to include them, is the sin which Christ said could find no forgiveness.

I had a personal instance of this the other day which illustrates so clearly what I mean that I will quote it. I wrote a book called *The Child of the Dawn*, the point of which was to represent, in an allegory, my sincere belief that the after-life of man must be a life of effort, and experience, and growth. A lady wrote me a very discourteous letter to say that she believed the after-life to be one of Rest, and that she held what she believed to be my view to be unchristian and untrue. The notion that ardent, loving, eager spirits should be required to spend eternity in a sort of lazy contentment, forbidden to stir a finger for love and truth and right, is surely an insupportable one! What would be the joy of heaven to a soul full of energy and love, condemned to such luxurious apathy, forced to drowse through the ages in epicurean ease? If heaven has any meaning at all, it must satisfy our best and most active aspirations; and a paradise of utter and eternal indolence would be purgatory or hell to all noble natures. But this poor creature, tired no doubt by life and its anxieties, overcome by dreariness and sorrow, was not only desirous of solitary and profound repose, but determined to impose her own theory upon all the world as well. I blame no one for desiring rest; but to wish, as she made no secret that she wished, to crush and confound one who thought and hoped otherwise, does seem to me a very mean and wretched point of view. That, alas, is what many people mean when they say that they *believe* a thing, namely that they would be personally annoyed if it turned out to be different from what they hoped.

I am sure that we ought rather to welcome with all our might any evidence of strength and energy and joy, even if they seem to spring from principles entirely opposite to our own. The more we know of men and women, the more we ought to perceive that half the trouble in the world comes from our calling the same principles by different names. We are not called upon to give up our own principles, but we must beware of trying to meddle with the principles of other people.

And therefore we must never be disturbed and still less annoyed by other people finding fault with our tastes and principles, calling them fantastic and sentimental, weak and affected, so long as they do not seek to impose their own beliefs upon us. That they should do so is of course a mistake; but we must recognise that it comes either from the stupidity which is the result of a lack of sympathy, or else from the nobler error of holding an opinion strongly and earnestly. We must never be betrayed into making the same mistake; we may try to persuade, and it is better done by example than by argument, but we must never allow ourselves to scoff and deride, and still less to abuse and vilify. We must rather do our best to understand the other point of view, and to acquiesce in the possibility of its being held, even if we cannot understand it. We must take for granted that every one whose life shows evidence of energy, unselfishness, joyfulness, ardour, peacefulness, is truly inspired by the spirit of good. We must believe that they have a vision of beauty and delight, born of the spirit. We must rejoice if they are making plain to other minds any interpretation of life, any enrichment of motive, any protest against things coarse and low and mean. We may wish — and we may try to persuade them — that their hopes and aims were wider, more bountiful, and more inclusive, but if we seek to exclude those hopes and aims, however inconsistent they may be with our own, that moment the shadow involves our own hopes, because our desire must be that the world may somehow become happier, fuller, more joyful, even if it is not on the lines which we ourselves approve.

I know so many good people who are anxious to increase happiness, but only on their own conditions; they feel that they estimate exactly what the quantity and quality of joy ought to be, and they treat the joy which they do not themselves feel as an offence against truth. It is from these beliefs, I have often thought, that much of the unhappiness of family circles arises, the elders not realising how the world moves on, how new ideas come to the front, how the old hopes fade or are transmuted. They see their children liking different thoughts, different occupations, new books, new pleasures; and instead of trying to enter into these things, to believe in their innocence and their naturalness, they try to crush and thwart them, with the result that the boys and girls just hide their feelings and desires, and if they are not shamed out of them, which sometimes happens, they hold them secretly and half sullenly, and plan how to escape as soon as they can from the tender and anxious constraint into a real world of their own. And the saddest part of all is that the younger generation learn no experience thus; but when they form a circle of their own and the same expansion happens, they do as their parents did, saying to themselves, "My parents lost my confidence by insisting on what was not really important; but *my* objections are reasonable and justifiable, and my children must trust me to know what is right."

We must realise then that elasticity and sympathy are the first of duties, and that if we embark upon the crusade of joy, we must do it expecting to find many kinds of joy at work in the world, and some which we cannot understand. We may of course mistrust destructive joy, the joy of selfish pleasure, rough combativeness, foolish wastefulness, ugly riot — all the joys that are evidently dogged by sorrow and pain; but if we see any joy that leads to self-restraint and energy and usefulness and activity, we must recognise it as divine.

We may have then our private fancies, our happy pursuits, our sweet delights; we may practise them, sure that the best proof of their energy is that they obviously and plainly increase and multiply our own happiness. But if we direct others at all, it must be as a signpost, pointing to a parting of roads and making the choice clear, and not as a policeman enforcing the majesty of our self-invented laws.

Everything that helps us, invigorates us, comforts us, sustains us, gives us life, is right for us; of that we need never be in any doubt, provided always that our delight is not won at the expense of others; and we must allow and encourage exactly the same liberty in others to choose their own rest, their own pleasure, their own refreshment. What would one think of a host, whose one object was to make his guests eat and drink and do exactly what he himself enjoyed? And yet that is precisely what many of the most conscientious people are doing all day long, in other regions of the soul and mind.

The one thing which we have to fear, in all this, is of lapsing into indolence and solitary enjoyment, guarding and hoarding our own happiness. We must measure the effectiveness of our enjoyment by one thing and one thing alone — our increase of affection and sympathy, our interest in other minds and lives. If we only end by desiring to be apart from it all, to gnaw the meat we have torn from life in a secret cave of our devising, to gain serenity by indifference, then we must put our desires aside; but if it sends us into the world with hope and energy and interest and above all affection, then we need have no anxiety; we may enter like the pilgrims into comfortable houses of refreshment, where we can look with interest at pictures and spiders and poultry and all the pleasant wonders of the place; we may halt in wayside arbours to taste cordials and confections, and enjoy from the breezy hill-top the pleasant vale of Beulah, with the celestial mountains rising blue and still upon the far horizon.

XIX
SCIENCE

I read the other day a very downright book, with a kind of dry insolence about it, by a man who was concerned with stating what he called the *mechanistic* theory of the universe. The worlds, it seemed, were like a sandy desert, with a wind that whirled the sands about; and indeed I seemed, as I looked out on the world through the writer's eyes, to see nothing but wind and sand! One of his points was that every thought that passed through the mind was preceded by a change in the particles of the brain; so that philosophy, and religion, and life itself were nothing but a shifting of the sand by the impalpable wind — matter and motion, that was all! Again and again he said, in his dry way, that no theory was of any use that was not supported by facts; and that though there was left a little corner of thought, which was still unexplained, we should soon have some more facts, and the last mystery would be hunted down.

But it seemed to me, as I read it, that the thoughts of man were just as much facts as any other facts, and that when a man had a vision of beauty, or when a hope came to him in a bitter sorrow, it was just as real a thing as the little particle of the brain which stirred and crept nearer to another particle. I do not say that all theories of religion and philosophy are necessarily true, but they are real enough; they have existed, they exist, they cannot die. Of course, in making out a theory, we must not neglect one set of facts and depend wholly on another set of facts; but I believe that the intense and pathetic desire of humanity to know why they are here, why they feel as they do, why they suffer and rejoice, what awaits them, are facts just as significant as the blood that drips from the wound, or the leaf that unfolds in the sun. The comforting and uplifting conclusion which the writer came to was that we were just a set of animated puppets, spun out of the drift of sand and dew by the thing that he called force. But if that is so, why are we not all perfectly complacent and contented, why do we love and grieve and wish to be different? I do still believe that there is a spirit that mingles with our hopes and dreams, something personal, beautiful, fatherly, pure, something which is unwillingly tied to earth and would be free if it could. The sense that we are ourselves wholly separate and distinct, with experience behind us and experience before us, seems to me a fact beside which all other facts pale into insignificance. And next in strength to that seems the fact that we can recognise, and draw near to, and be amazingly desirous of, as well as no less strangely hostile to, other similar selves; that our thought can mingle with theirs, pass into theirs, as theirs into ours, forging a bond which no accident of matter can dissolve.

Does it really satisfy the lover, when he knows that his love is answered, to realise that it is all the result of some preceding molecular action of the brain? That does not seem to me so much a truculent statement as a foolish statement, shirking, like a glib and silly child, the most significant of data. And I think we shall do well to say to our scientist, as courteously as Sir Lancelot said to the officious knight, who proffered unnecessary service, that we have no need for him at this time.

Now, I am not saying, in all this, that the investigation of science is wrong or futile. It is exactly the reverse; the message of God is hidden in all the minutest material things that lie about us; and it is a very natural and even noble work to explore it; but it is wrong if it leads us to draw any conclusions at present beyond what we can reasonably and justly draw. It is the inference that what explains the visible scheme of things can also explain the invisible. That is wrong!

Let me here quote a noble sentence, which has often given me much-needed help, and served to remind me that thought is after all as real a thing as matter, when I have been tempted to feel otherwise. It was written by a very wise and tender philosopher, William James, who was never betrayed by his own severe standard of truth and reality into despising the common dreams and aspirations of simpler men. He wrote:

"I find it preposterous to suppose that if there be a feeling of unseen reality, shared by numbers of the best men in their best moments, responded to by other men in their deep moments, good to live by, strength-giving — I find it preposterous, I say, to suppose that the goodness of that feeling for living purposes should be held to carry no objective significance, and especially preposterous if it combines harmoniously with an otherwise grounded philosophy of objective truth."

That is a very large and tolerant utterance, both in its suspension of impatient certainties and in its beautiful sympathy with all ardent visions that cannot clearly and convincingly find logical utterance.

What I am trying to say in this little book is not addressed to professional philosophers or men of science, who are concerned with intellectual investigation, but to those who have to live life as it is, as the vast majority of men must always be. What I rather beg of them is not to be alarmed and bewildered by the statements either of scientific or religious dogmatists. No doubt we should like to know everything, to have all our perplexities resolved; but we have reached that point neither in religion nor in philosophy, nor even in science. We must be content not to know. But because we do not know, we need not therefore refuse to feel; there is no excuse for us to thrust the whole tangle away and out of sight, and just to do as far as possible what we like. We may admire and hope and love, and it is our business to do all three. The thing that seems to me — and I am here only stating a personal view — both possible and desirable, is to live as far as we can by the law of beauty, not to submit to anything by which our soul is shamed and insulted, not to be drawn into strife, not to fall into miserable fault-finding, not to allow ourselves to be fretted and fussed and agitated by the cares of life; but to say clearly to ourselves, "that is a petty, base, mean thought, and I will not entertain it; this is a generous and kind and gracious thought, and I will welcome it and obey it."

One of the clearly discernible laws of life is that we can both check and contract habits; and when we begin our day, we can begin it if we will by prayer and aspiration and resolution, as much as we can begin it with bath and toilet. We can say, "I will live resolutely today in joy and good-humour and energy and kindliness." Those powers and possibilities are all there; and even if we are overshadowed by disappointment and anxiety and pain, we can say to ourselves that we will behave as if it were not so; because there is undoubtedly a very real and noble pleasure in putting off shadows and troubles, and not letting them fall in showers on those about us. We need not be stoical or affectedly bright; we often cannot give those who love us greater joy than to tell them of our troubles and let them comfort us. And we can be practical too in our outlook, because much of the grittiest irritation of life is caused by indulging indolence when we ought not, and being hurried when we might be leisurely. It is astonishing how a little planning will help us in all this, and how soon a habit is set up. We do not, it is true, know the limits of our power of choice. But the illusion, if it be an illusion, that we have a power of choice, is an infinitely more real fact to most of us than the molecular motion of the brain particles.

And then too there is another fact, which is becoming more and more clear, namely, what is called the power of suggestion. That if we can put a thought into our mind, not into our reason, but into our inner mind of instinct and force, whether it be a base thought or a noble thought, it seems to soak unconsciously into the very stuff of the mind, and keep reproducing itself even when we seem to have forgotten all about it. And this is, I believe, one of the uses of prayer, that we put a thought into the mind, which can abide with us, secretly it may be, all the day; and that thus it is not a mere pious habit or tradition to have a quiet period at the beginning of the day, in which we can nurture some joyful and generous hope, but as real a source of strength to the spirit as the morning meal is to the body. I have myself found that it is well, if one can, to read a fragment of some fine, generous, beautiful, or noble-minded book at such an hour.

There is in many people who work hard with their brains a curious and unreal mood of sadness which hangs about the waking hour, which I have thought to be a sort of hunger of the mind, craving to be fed; and this is accompanied, at least in me, by a very swift, clear, and hopeful apprehension, so that a beautiful thought comes to me as a draught of water to a thirsty man. So I make haste, as often as may be, just to drop such a thought at those times into the mind; it falls to the depths, as one may see a bright coin go gleaming and shifting down to the depths of a pool; or to use a homelier similitude, like sugar that drops to the bottom of a cup, sweetening the draught.

These are little homely things; but it is through simple use and not through large theory that one can best practise joy.

XX

WORK

I came out of the low-arched door with a sense of relief and passed into the sunshine; the meeting had broken up, and we went our ways. We had sate there an hour or two in the old panelled room, a dozen full-blooded friendly men discussing a small matter with wonderful ingenuity and zest; and I had spoken neither least nor most mildly, and had found it all pleasant enough. Then I mounted my bicycle and rode out into the fragrant country alone, with all its nearer green and further blue; there in that little belt of space, between the thin air above and the dense-dark earth beneath, was the pageant of conscious life enacting itself so visibly and eagerly. In the sunlit sky the winds raced gaily enough, with the void silence of moveless space above it; below my feet what depths of cold stone, with the secret springs; below that perhaps a core of molten heat and imprisoned fire!

What was it all about? What were we all doing there? What was the significance of the little business that had been engaging our minds and tongues? What part did it play in the mighty universe?

The thorn-tree thick with bloom, pouring out its homely spicy smell — it was doing too, beautifully enough, what we had been doing clumsily. It was living, intent on its own conscious life, the sap hurrying, the scent flowing, the bud waxing. The yellow-hammer poising and darting along the hedge, the sparrow twittering round the rick, the cock picking and crowing, were all intent on life, proclaiming that they were alive and busy. Something vivid, alert, impassioned was going forward everywhere, something being effected, something uttered — and yet the cause how utterly hidden from me and from every living thing!

The memory of old poetry began to flicker in my mind like summer lightning. In the orchard, crammed with bloom, two unseen children were calling to each other; a sunburned, careless, graceful boy, whose rough clothes could not conceal his shapely limbs and easy movements, came driving some cows along the lane. He asked me the time in Dorian speech. The shepherds piping together on the Sicilian headland could not have made a fairer picture; and yet the boy and I could hardly have had a thought in common!

All the poets that ever sang in the pleasant springtime can hardly have felt the joyful onrush of the season more sweetly than I felt it that day; and yet no philosopher or priest could have given me a hint of what the mystery was, why so ceaselessly renewed; but it was clear to me at least that the mind behind it was joyful enough, and wished me to share its joy.

And then an hour later I was doing for no reason but that it was my business the dullest of tasks — no less than revising a whole sheaf of the driest of examination papers. Elaborate questions to elicit knowledge of facts arid and meaningless, which it was worth no human being's while to know, unless he could fill out the bare outlines with some of the stuff of life. Hundreds of boys, I dare say, in crowded schoolrooms all over the country were having those facts drummed into them, with no aim in sight but the answering of the questions which I was manipulating. That was a bewildering business, that we should insist on that sort of drilling becoming a part of life. Was that a relation it was well to establish? As the fine old, shrewd, indolent Dr. Johnson said, he for his part, while he lived, never again desired even to hear of the Punic War! And again he said, "You teach your daughters the diameters of the planets, and wonder, when you have done, why they do not desire your company."

Cannot we somehow learn to simplify life? Must we continue to think that we can inspire children in rows? Is it not possible for us to be a little less important and pompous and elaborate about it all, to aim at more direct relations, to say more what we feel, to do more what nature bids us do?

The heart sickens at the thought of how we keep to the grim highways of life, and leave the pleasant spaces of wood and field unvisited! And all because we want more than we need, and because we cannot be content unless we can be envied and admired.

The cure for all this, it seems to me, is a resolute avoidance of complications and intricacies, a determination to live life more on our own terms, and to open our eyes to the simpler pleasures which lie waiting in our way on every side.

I do not believe in the elaborate organisation of life; and yet I think it is possible to live in the midst of it, and yet not to be involved in it. I do not believe in fierce rebellion, but I do believe in quiet transformation; and here comes in the faith that I have in *Joyous Gard*. I believe that day by day we should clear a space to live with minds that have felt, and hoped, and enjoyed. That is the first duty of all; and then that we should live in touch with the natural beauty of the earth, and let the sweetness of it enter into our minds and hearts; for then we come out renewed, to find the beauty and the fulness of life in the hearts and minds of those about us. Life is complicated, not because its issues are not simple enough, but because we are most of us so afraid of a phantom which we create — the criticism of other human beings.

If one reads the old books of chivalry, there seems an endless waste of combat and fighting among men who had the same cause at heart, and who yet for the pettiest occasions of dispute must need try to inflict death on each other, each doing his best to shatter out of the world another human being who loved life as well. Two doughty knights, Sir Lamorak and Sir Meliagraunce, must needs hew pieces off each other's armour, break each other's bones, spill each other's blood, to prove which of two ladies is the fairer; and when it is all over, nothing whatever is proved about the ladies, nothing but which of the two knights is the stronger! And yet we seem to be doing the same thing to this day, except that we now try to wound the heart and mind, to make a fellow man afraid and suspicious, to take the light out of his day and the energy out of his work. For the last few weeks a handful of earnest clergymen have been endeavouring in a Church paper, with floods of pious Billingsgate, to make me ridiculous about a technical question of archæological interest, and all because my opinion differs from their own! I thankfully confess that as I get older, I care not at all for such foolish controversy, and the only qualms I have are the qualms I feel at finding human beings so childish and so fretful.

Well, it is all very curious, and not without its delight too! What I earnestly desire is that men and women should not thus waste precious time and pleasant life, but go straight to reality, to hope. There are a hundred paths that can be trodden; only let us be sure that we are treading our own path, not feebly shifting from track to track, not following too much the bidding of others, but knowing what interests us, what draws us, what we love and desire; and above all keeping in mind that it is our business to understand and admire and conciliate each other, whether we do it in a panelled room, with pens and paper on the table, and the committee in full cry; or out on the quiet road, with one whom we trust entirely, where the horizon runs, field by field and holt by holt, to meet the soft verge of encircling sky.

XXI
HOPE

The other day I took up idly some magazine or other, one of those great lemon-coloured, salmon-hued, slaty paper volumes which lie in rows on the tables of my club. I will not stop now to enquire why English taste demands covers which show every mean stain, every soiled finger-print; but these volumes are always a reproach to me, because they show me, alas! how many subjects, how many methods of presenting subjects, are wholly uninteresting and unattractive to my trivial mind. This time, however, my eye fell upon a poem full of light and beauty, and of that subtle grace which seems so incomprehensible, so uncreated — a lyric by Mr. Alfred Noyes. It was like a spell which banished for an instant the weariness born of a long, hot, tedious committee, the oppression which always falls on me at the sight and sound of the cataract of human beings and vehicles, running so fiercely in the paved channels of London. A beautiful poem, but how immeasurably sad, an invocation to the memory and to the spirit of Robert Browning, not speaking of him in an elegiac strain as of a great poet who had lived his life to the full and struck his clear-toned harp, solemnly, sweetly, and whimsically too, year after year; but as of something great and noble wholly lost and separated from the living world.

This was a little part of it:

> *Singer of hope for all the world,*
> *Is it still morning where thou art,*
> *Or are the clouds that hide thee furled*
> *Around a dark and silent heart?*
>
> *The sacred chords thy hand could wake*
> *Are fallen on utter silence here,*
> *And hearts too little even to break*
> *Have made an idol of despair.*
>
> *Come back to England, where thy May*
> *Returns, but not that rapturous light;*
> *God is not in His heaven today,*
> *And with thy country nought is right.*

I think that almost magically beautiful! But is it true? I hope not and I think not. The poet went on to say that Paradox had destroyed the sanctity of Truth, and that Science had done nothing more than strip the skeleton of the flesh and blood that vested it, and crown the anatomy with glory. One cannot speak more severely, more gloomily, of an age than to say that it is deceived by analysis and paradox, and cares nothing for nobler and finer things. It seems to me to be a sorrowful view of life that, to have very little faith or prospect about it. It is true indeed that the paradox-maker is popular now; but that is because men are interested in interpretations of life; and it is true too that we are a little impatient now of fancy and imagination, and want to get at facts, because we feel that fancy and imagination, which are not built on facts, are very tricksy guides to life. But the view seems to me both depressed and morbid which cannot look beyond, and see that the world is passing on in its own great unflinching, steady manner. It is like the view of a child who, confronted with a pain, a disagreeable incident, a tedious day of drudgery, wails that it can never be happy again.

The poem ends with a fine apostrophe to Browning as one "who stormed through death, and laid hold of Eternity." Did he indeed do that? I wish I felt it! He had, of course, an unconquerable optimism, which argued promise from failure and perfection from incompleteness. But I cannot take such hopes on the word of another, however gallant and noble he may be. I do not want hopes which are only within the reach of the vivid and high-hearted; the crippled, drudging slave cannot rejoice because he sees his warrior-lord gay, heroic, and strong. I must build my creed on my own hopes and possibilities, not on the strength and cheerfulness of another.

And then my eye fell on a sentence opposite, out of an article on our social problems; and this was what I read:

" . . . the tears of a hunger-bitten philosophy, which is so appalled by the common doom of man — that he must eat his bread by the sweat of his brow — that it can talk, write, and think of nothing else."

I think there is more promise in that, rough and even rude as the statement is, because it opens up a real hope for something that is coming, and is not a mere lamentation over a star that is set.

"A hunger-bitten philosophy" — is it not rather that there is creeping into the world an uneasy sense that we must, if we are to be happy, *share* our happiness? It is not that the philosopher is hungry, it is that he cannot bear to think of all the other people who are condemned to hunger; and why it occupies his tongue and his pen, is that it clouds his serenity to know that others cannot now be serene. All this unrest, this grasping at the comfort of life on the one hand,

and the patience, the justice, the tolerance, with which such claims are viewed by many possessors on the other, is because there is a spirit of sympathy growing up, which has not yet become self-sacrifice, but is on its way to become so.

Then we must ask ourselves what our duty is. Not, I think, with all our comforts about us, to chant loud odes about its being all right with the world, but to see what we can do to make it all right, to equalise, to share, to give.

The finest thing, of course, would be if those who are set in the midst of comfort could come calmly out of it, and live simpler, kinder, more direct lives; but apart from that, what can we do? Is it our duty, in the face of all that, to surrender every species of enjoyment and delight, to live meanly and anxiously because others have to live so? I am not at all sure that it would not prove our greatness if the thought of all the helpless pain and drudgery of the world, the drift of falling tears, were so intolerable to us that we simply could not endure the thought; but I think that would end in quixotism and pessimism of the worst kind, if one would not eat or drink, because men starve in Russia or India, if one would not sleep because sufferers toss through the night in pain. That seems a morbid and self-sought suffering.

No, I believe that we must share our joy as far as we can, and that it is our duty rather to have joy to share, and to guard the quality of it, make it pure and true. We do best if we can so refine our happiness as to make it a thing which is not dependent upon wealth or ease; and the more natural our life is, the more can we be of use by the example which is not self-conscious but contagious, by showing that joy does not depend upon excitement and stimulus, but upon vivid using of the very stuff of life.

Where we fail, many of us, is in the elaborateness of our pleasures, in the fact that we learn to be connoisseurs rather than viveurs, in losing our taste for the ancient wholesome activities and delights.

I had caught an hour, that very day, to visit the Academy; it was a doubtful pleasure, though if I could have had the great rooms to myself it would have been a delightful thing enough; but to be crushed and elbowed by such numbers of people who seemed intent not on looking at anything, but on trying to see if they could recognise any of their friends! It was a curious collection certainly! So many pictures of old disgraceful men, whose faces seemed like the faces of toads or magpies; dull, blinking, malign, or with the pert brightness of acquisition. There were pictures too of human life so-called, silly, romantic, insincerely posed; some fatuous allegorical things, like ill-staged melodramas; but the strength of English art came out for all that in the lovely landscapes, rich fields, summer streams, far-off woodlands, beating seas; and I felt in looking at it all that the pictures which moved one most were those which gave one a sudden hunger for the joy and beauty of earth, not ill-imagined fantastic places, but scenes that one has looked upon a hundred times with love and contentment, the corn-field, the mill with its brimming leat, the bathing-place among quiet pastures, the lake set deep in water-plants, the old house in the twilight garden — all the things consecrated throughout long ages by use and life and joy.

And then I strayed into the sculpture gallery; and I cannot describe the thrill which half a dozen of the busts there gave me — faces into which the wonder and the love and the pain of life seemed to have passed, and which gave me a sudden sense of that strange desire to claim a share in the past and present and future of the form and face in which one suddenly saw so much to love. One seemed to feel hands held out; hearts crying for understanding and affection, breath on one's cheek, words in one's ears; and thus the whole gallery melted into a great throng of signalling and beckoning presences, the air dense with the voices of spirits calling to me, pressing upon me; offering and claiming love, all bound upon one mysterious pilgrimage, none able to linger or to stay, and yet willing to clasp one close by the roadside, in wonder at the marvellous inscrutable power behind it all, which at the same moment seemed to say, "Rest here, love, be loved, enjoy," and at the same moment cried, "Go forward, experience, endure, lament, come to an end."

There again opened before one the awful mystery of the beauty and the grief of life, the double strain which we must somehow learn to combine, the craving for continuance, side by side with the knowledge of interruption and silence. If one is real, the other cannot be real! And I for one have no doubt of which reality I hold to. Death and silence may deceive us; life and joy cannot. There may be something hidden beneath the seeming termination of mortal experience; indeed, I fully believe that there is; but even if it were not so, nothing could make love and joy unreal, or destroy the consciousness of what says within us, "This Is I." Our one hope then is not to be deceived or beguiled or bewildered by the complexity and intricacy of life; the path of each of us lies clear and direct through the tangle.

And thus, as I have said, our task is not to be defrauded of our interior peace. No power that we know can do more than dissolve and transmute our mortal frame; it can melt into the earth, it can be carried into the depths of the sea, but it cannot be annihilated; and this is infinitely more true of our spirits; they may undergo a thousand transformations and transmutations, but they must be eternally there.

So let us claim our experience bravely and accept it firmly, never daunted by it, never utterly despairing, leaping back into life and happiness as swiftly as we can, never doubting that it is assured to us. The time that we waste is that which is spent in anxious, trivial, conventional things. We have to bear them in our burdens, many of us, but do not let us be for ever examining them, weighing them in our hands, wishing them away, whining over them; we must not let them beguile us of the better part. If the despairing part of us cries out that it is frightened, wearied, anxious, we must not heed it; we must again and again assure ourselves that the peace is there, and that we miss it by our own fault. Above all let us not make pitiable excuses for ourselves. We must be like the woman in the parable who, when she lost the coin, did not sit down to bewail her ill-luck, but swept the house diligently until she found it. There is no such thing as loss in the world; what we lose is merely withheld until we have earned the right to find it again. We must not cultivate repentance, we must not yield to remorse. The only thing worth having is a wholesome sorrow for not having done better; but it is ignoble to remember, if our remembrance has anything hopeless about it; and we do best utterly to forget our failures and lapses, because of this we may be wholly sure, that joys are restored to us, that strength returns, and that peace beyond measure is waiting for us; and not only waiting for us, but as near us as a closed door in the room in which we sit. We can rise up, we can turn thither, we can enter if we will and when we will.

XXII
EXPERIENCE

It is very strange to contemplate the steady plunge of good advice, like a cataract of ice-cold water, into the brimming and dancing pool of youth and life, the maxims of moralists and sages, the epigrams of cynics, the sermons of priests, the good-humoured warnings of sensible men, all crying out that nothing is really worth the winning, that fame brings weariness and anxiety, that love is a fitful fever, that wealth is a heavy burden, that ambition is a hectic dream; to all of which ejaculations youth does not listen and cannot listen, but just goes on its eager way, trying its own experiments, believing in the delight of triumph and success, determined, at all events, to test all for itself. All this confession of disillusionment and disappointment is true, but only partially true. The struggle, the effort, the perseverance, does bring fine things with it — things finer by far than the shining crown and the loud trumpets that attend it.

The explanation of it seems to be that men require to be tempted to effort, by the dream of fame and wealth and leisure and imagined satisfaction. It is the experience that we need, though we do not know it; and experience, by itself, seems such a tedious, dowdy, tattered thing, like a flag burnt by sun, bedraggled by rain, torn by the onset, that it cannot by itself prove attractive. Men are heavily preoccupied with ends and aims, and the recognised values of the objects of desire and hope are often false and distorted values. So singularly constituted are we, that the hope of idleness is alluring, and some people are early deceived into habits of idleness, because they cannot know what it is that lies on the further side of work. Of course the bodily life has to be supplied, but when a man has all that he needs — let us say food and drink, a quiet shelter, a garden and a row of trees, a grassy meadow with a flowing stream, a congenial task, a household of his own — it seems not enough! Let us suppose all that granted to a man: he must consider next what kind of life he has gained; he has the cup in his hands; with what liquor is it to be filled? That is the point at which the imagination of man seems to fail; he cannot set himself to vigorous, wholesome life for its own sake. He has to be ever looking past it and beyond it for something to yield him an added joy.

Now, what we all have to do, if we can, is to regard life steadily and generously, to see that life, experience, emotion, are the real gifts; not things to be hurried through, thrust aside, disregarded, as a man makes a hasty meal before some occasion that excites him. One must not use life like the passover feast, to be eaten with loins girded and staff in hand. It is there to be lived, and what we have to do is to make the quality of it as fine as we can.

We must provide then, if we can, a certain setting for life, a sufficiency of work and sustenance, and even leisure; and then we must give that no further thought. How many men do I not know, whose thought seems to be "when I have made enough money, when I have found my place, when I have arranged the apparatus of life about me, then I will live as I should wish to live." But the stream of desires broadens and thickens, and the leisure hour never comes!

We must not thus deceive ourselves. What we have to do is to make life, instantly and without delay, worthy to be lived. We must try to enjoy all that we have to do, and take care that we do not do what we do not enjoy, unless the hard task we set ourselves is sure to bring us something that we really need. It is useless thus to elaborate the cup of life, if we find when we have made it, that the wine which should have filled it has long ago evaporated.

Can I say what I believe the wine of life to be? I believe that it is a certain energy and richness of spirit, in which both mind and heart find full expression. We ought to rise day by day with a certain zest, a clear intention, a design to make the most out of every hour; not to let the busy hours shoulder each other, tread on each other's heels, but to force every action to give up its strength and sweetness. There is work to be done, and there are empty hours to be filled as well. It is happiest of all, for man and woman, if those hours can be filled, not as a duty but as a pleasure, by pleasing those whom we love and whose nearness is at once a delight. We ought to make time for that most of all. And then there ought to be some occupation, not enforced, to which we naturally wish to return. Exercise, gardening, handicraft, writing, even if it be only leisurely letters, music, reading — something to occupy the restless brain and hand; for there is no doubt that both physically and mentally we are not fit to be unoccupied.

But most of all, there must be something to quicken, enliven, practise the soul. We must not force this upon ourselves, or it will be fruitless and dreary; but neither must we let it lapse out of mere indolence. We must follow some law of beauty, in whatever way beauty appeals to us and calls us. We must not think that appeal a selfish thing, because it is upon that and that alone that our power of increasing peace and hope and vital energy belongs.

I have a man in mind who has a simple taste for books. He has a singularly pure and fine power of selecting and loving what is best in books. There is no self-consciousness about him, no critical contempt of the fancies of others; but his own love for what is beautiful is so modest, so perfectly natural and unaffected, that it is impossible to hear him speak of the things that he loves without a desire rising up in one's mind to taste a pleasure which brings so much happiness to the owner. I have often talked with him about books that I had thought tiresome and dull; but he disentangles so deftly the underlying idea of the book, the thought that one must be on the look-out for the motive of the whole, that he has again and again sent me back to a book which I had thrown aside, with an added interest and perception. But the really notable thing is the effect on his own immediate circle. I do not think his family are naturally people of very high intelligence or ability. But his mind and heart seem to have permeated theirs, so that I know no group of persons who seem to have imbibed so simply, without strain or effort, a delight in what is good and profound. There is no sort of dryness about the atmosphere. It is not that they keep talk resolutely on their own subjects; it is merely that their outlook is so fresh and quick that everything seems alive and significant. One comes away from the house with a horizon strangely extended, and a sense that the world is full of live ideas and wonderful affairs.

I despair of describing an effect so subtle, so contagious. It is not in the least that everything becomes intellectual; that would be a rueful consequence; there is no parade of knowledge, but knowledge itself becomes an exciting and entertaining thing, like a varied landscape. The wonder is, when one is with these people, that one did not see all the fine things that were staring one in the face all the time, the clues, the connections, the links. The best of it is that it is not a transient effect; it is rather like the implanting of a seed of fire, which spreads and glows, and burns unaided.

It is this sacred fire of which we ought all to be in search. Fire is surely the most wonderful symbol in the world! We sit in our quiet rooms, feeling safe, serene, even chilly, yet everywhere about us, peacefully confined in all our furniture and belongings, is a mass of inflammability, stored with gases, which at a touch are capable of leaping into flame. I remember once being in a house in which a pile of wood in a cellar had caught fire; there was a short delay, while the hose was got out, and before an aperture into the burning room could be made. I went into a peaceful dining-room, which was just above the fire, and it was strangely appalling to see little puffs of smoke fly off from the kindled floor, while we tore the carpets up and flew to take the pictures down, and to know the room was all crammed with vehement cells, ready to burst into vapour at the fierce touch of the consuming element.

I saw once a vast bonfire of wood kindled on a grassy hill-top; it was curiously affecting to see the great trunks melt into flame, and the red cataract pouring so softly, so unapproachably into the air. It is so with the minds of men; the material is all there, compressed, welded, inflammable; and if the fire can but leap into our spirits from some other burning heart, we may be amazed at the prodigal force and heat that can burst forth, the silent energy, the possibility of consumption.

I hold it to be of supreme value to each of us to try to introduce this fire of the heart into our spirits. It is not like mortal fire, a consuming, dangerous, truculent element. It is rather like the furnace of the engine, which can convert water into steam — the softest, feeblest, purest element into irresistible and irrepressible force. The materials are all at hand in many a spirit that has never felt the glowing contact; and it is our business first to see that the elements are there, and then to receive with awe the fiery touch. It must be restrained, controlled, guarded, that fierce conflagration; but our joy cannot only consist of pure, clear, lambent, quiescent elements. It must have a heart of flame.

XXIII
FAITH

We ought to learn to cultivate, train, regulate emotion, just as we train other faculties. The world has hardly reached this point yet. First man trains his body that he may be strong, when strength is supreme. When almost the only argument is force, the man who is drawn to play a fine part in the world must above everything be strong, courageous, gallant, so that he may go to combat joyful and serene, like a man inspired. Then when the world becomes civilised, when weakness combines against strength, when men do not settle differences of feeling by combat and war, but by peaceable devices like votes and arbitrations, the intellect comes to the front, and strength of body falls into the background as a pleasant enough thing, a matter of amusement or health, and intellect becomes the dominant force. But we shall advance beyond even that, and indeed we have begun to advance. Buddhism and the Stoic philosophy were movements dictated more by reason than by emotion, which recognised the elements of pain and sorrow as inseparable from human life, and suggested to man that the only way to conquer evils such as these was by turning the back upon them, cultivating indifference to them, and repressing the desires which issued in disappointment. Christianity was the first attempt of the human spirit to achieve a nobler conquest still; it taught men to abandon the idea of conquest altogether; the Christian was meant to abjure ambition, not to resist oppression, not to meet violence by violence, but to yield rather than to fight.

The metaphor of the Christian soldier is wholly alien to the spirit of the Gospel, and the attempt to establish a combative ideal of Christian life was one of the many concessions that Christianity in the hands of its later exponents made to the instincts of men. The conception of the Christian in the Gospel was that of a simple, uncomplicated, uncalculating being, who was to be so absorbed in caring for others that the sense of his own rights and desires and aims was to fall wholly into the background. He is not represented as meant to have any intellectual, political, or artistic pursuits at all. He is to accept his place in the world as he finds it; he is to have no use for money or comforts or accumulated resources. He is not to scheme for dignity or influence, nor even much to regard earthly ties. Sorrow, loss, pain, evil, are simply to be as shadows through which he passes, and if they have any meaning at all for him, they are to be opportunities for testing the strength of his emotions. But the whole spirit of the Christian revelation is that no terms should be made with the world at all. The world must treat the Christian as it will, and there are to be no reprisals; neither is there the least touch of opportunism about it. The Christian is not to do the best he can, but the best; he is frankly to aim at perfection.

How then is this faith to be sustained? It is to be nourished by a sense of direct and frank converse with a God and Father. The Christian is never to have any doubt that the intention of the Father towards him is absolutely, kind and good. He attempts no explanation of the existence of sin and pain; he simply endures them; and he looks forward with serene certainty to the continued existence of the soul. There is no hint given of the conditions under which the soul is to continue its further life, of its desires or occupations; the intention obviously is that a Christian should live life freely and fully; but love, and interest in human relations are to supersede all other aims and desires.

It has been often said that if the world were to accept the teaching of the Sermon on the Mount literally, the social fabric of the world would be dissolved in a month. It is true; but it is not generally added that it would be because there would be no need of the social fabric. The reason why the social fabric would be dissolved is because there would doubtless be a minority which would not accept these principles, and would seize upon the things which the world agrees to consider desirable. The Christian majority would become the slaves of the unchristian minority, and would be at their mercy. Christianity, in so far as it is a social system at all, is the purest kind of socialism, a socialism not of compulsion but of disinterestedness. It is easy, of course, to scoff at the possibility of so far disintegrating the vast and complex organisation of society, as to arrange life on the simpler lines; but the fact remains that the very few people in the world's history, like St. Francis of Assisi, for instance, who have ever dared to live literally in the Christian manner, have had an immeasurable effect upon the hearts and imaginations of the world. The truth is not that life cannot be so lived, but that humanity dares not take the plunge; and that is what Christ meant when He said that few would find the narrow way. The really amazing thing is that such immense numbers of people have accepted Christianity in the world, and profess themselves Christians without the slightest doubt of their sincerity, who never regard the Christian principles at all. The chief aim, it would seem, of the Church, has been not to preserve the original revelation, but to accommodate it to human instincts and desires. It seems to me to resemble the very quaint and simple old Breton legend, which relates how the Saviour sent the Apostles out to sell stale fish as fresh; and when they returned unsuccessful, He was angry with them, and said, "How shall I make you into fishers of men, if you cannot even persuade simple people to buy stale fish for fresh?" That is a very trenchant little allegory of ecclesiastical methods! And perhaps it is even so that it has come to pass that Christianity is in a sense a failure, or rather an unfulfilled hope, because it has made terms with the world, has become pompous and respectable and mundane and influential and combative, and has deliberately exalted civic duty above love.

It seems to me that it is the business of all serious Christians deliberately to face this fact; and equally it is not their business to try to destroy the social organisation of what is miscalled Christianity. That is as much a part of the world now as the Roman Empire was a part of the world when Christ came; but we must not mistake it for Christianity. Christianity is not a doctrine, or an organisation, or a ceremonial, or a society, but an atmosphere and a life. The essence of it is to train emotion, to believe and to practise the belief that all human beings have in them something interesting, lovable, beautiful, pathetic; and to make the recognition of that fact, the establishment of simple and kind relations with every single person with whom one is brought into contact, the one engrossing aim of life. Thus the essence of Christianity is in a sense artistic, because it depends upon freely recognising the beauty both of the natural world and the human spirit. There are enough hints of this in the Gospel, in the tender observation of Christ, His love of flowers, birds, children, the fact that He noted and reproduced in His stories the beauty of the homely business of life, the processes of husbandry in field and vineyard, the care of the sheepfold, the movement of the street, the games of boys and girls, the little festivals of life, the wedding and the party; all these things appear in His talk, and if more of it were recorded, there would undoubtedly be more of such things. It is true that as opposition and strife gathered about Him, there falls a darker and sadder spirit upon the page, and the anxieties and ambitions of His followers reflect themselves in the record of denunciations and censures. But we must not be misled by this into thinking that the message is thus obscured.

What then we have to do, if we would follow the pure Gospel, is to lead quiet lives, refresh the spirit of joy within us by feeding our eyes and minds with the beautiful sounds and sights of nature, the birds' song, the opening faces of flowers, the spring woods, the winter sunset; we must enter simply and freely into the life about us, not seeking to take a lead, to impress our views, to emphasise our own subjects; we must not get absorbed in toil or business, and still less in plans and intrigues; we must not protest against these things, but simply not care for them; we must not be burdensome to others in any way; we must not be shocked or offended or disgusted, but tolerate, forgive, welcome, share. We must treat life in an eager, light-hearted way, not ruefully or drearily or solemnly. The old language in which the Gospel comes to us, the formality of the antique phrasing, the natural tendency to make it dignified and hieratic, disguise from us how utterly natural and simple it all is. I do not think that reverence and tradition and awe have done us any more grievous injury than the fact that we have made the Saviour into a figure with whom frank communication, eager, impulsive talk, would seem to be impossible. One thinks of Him, from pictures and from books, as grave, abstracted, chiding, precise, mournfully kind, solemnly considerate. I believe it in my heart to have been wholly otherwise, and I think of Him as one with whom any simple and affectionate person, man, woman, or child, would have been entirely and instantly at ease. Like all idealistic and poetical natures, he had little use, I think, for laughter; those who are deeply interested in life and its issues care more for the beauty than the humour of life. But one sees a flash of humour here and there, as in the story of the unjust judge, and of the children in the market-place; and that He was disconcerting or cast a shadow upon natural talk and merriment I do not for an instant believe.

And thus I think that the Christian has no right to be ashamed of light-heartedness; indeed I believe that he ought to cultivate and feed it in every possible way. He ought to be so unaffected, that he can change without the least incongruity from laughter to tears, sympathising with, entering into, developing the moods of those about him. The moment that the Christian feels himself to be out of place and affronted by scenes of common resort — the market, the bar, the smoking-room — that moment his love of humanity fails him. He must be charming, attractive, genial, everywhere; for the severance of goodness and charm is a most wretched matter; if he affects his company at all, it must be as innocent and beautiful girlhood affects a circle, by its guilelessness, its sweetness, its appeal. I have known Christians like this, wise, beloved, simple, gentle people, whose presence did not bring constraint but rather a perfect ease, and was an evocation of all that was best and finest in those near them. I am not recommending a kind of silly mildness, interested only in improving conversation, but rather a zest, a shrewdness, a bonhomie, not finding natural interests common and unclean, but passionately devoted to human nature — so impulsive, frail, unequal, irritable, pleasure-loving, but yet with that generous, sweet, wholesome fibre below, that seems to be evoked in crisis and trial from the most apparently worthless human beings. The outcasts of society, the sinful, the ill-regulated, would never have so congregated about our Saviour if they had felt Him to be shocked or indignant at sin. What they must rather have felt was that He understood them, loved them, desired their love, and drew out all the true and fine and eager and lovable part of them, because he knew it to be there, wished it to emerge. "He was such a comfortable person!" as a simple man once said to me of one of the best of Christians: "if you had gone wrong, he did not find fault, but tried to see the way out; and if you were in pain or trouble, he said very little; you only felt it was all right when he was by."

XXIV
PROGRESS

We must always hopefully and gladly remember that the great movements, doctrines, thoughts, which have affected the life of the world most deeply, are those which are most truly based upon the best and truest needs of humanity. We need never be afraid of a new theory or a new doctrine, because such things are never imposed upon an unwilling world, but owe their strength to the closeness with which they interpret the aims and wants of human beings. Still more hopeful is the knowledge which one gains from looking back at the history of the world, that no selfish, cruel, sensual, or wicked interpretation of life has ever established a vital hold upon men. The selfish and the cruel elements of humanity have never been able to band themselves together against the power of good for very long, for the simple reason that those who are selfish and evil have a natural suspicion of other selfish and evil people; and no combination of men can ever be based upon anything but mutual trust and affection. And thus good has always a power of combination, while evil is naturally solitary and disjunctive.

Take such an attempt as that of Nietzsche to establish a new theory of life. His theory of the superman is simply this, that the future of the world was in the hands of strong, combative, powerful, predatory people. Those are the supermen, a natural aristocracy of force and unscrupulousness and vigour. But such individuals carry with them the seed of their own failure, because even if Nietzsche's view that the weak and broken elements of humanity were doomed to perish, and ought even to be helped to perish, were a true view, even if his supermen at last survived, they must ultimately be matched one against another in some monstrous and unflinching combat.

Nietzsche held that the Christian doctrine of renunciation was but a translating into terms of a theory the discontent, the disappointment, the failure of the weak and diseased element of humanity, the slavish herd. He thought that Christianity was a glorification, a consecration of man's weakness and not of his strength. But he misjudged it wholly. It is based in reality upon the noble element in humanity, the power of love and trust and unselfishness which rises superior to the ills of life; and the force of Christianity lies in the fact that it reveals to men the greatness of which they are capable, and the fact that no squalor or wretchedness of circumstances can bind the thought of man, if it is set upon what is high and pure. The man or woman who sees the beauty of inner purity cannot ever be very deeply tainted by corruption either of body or of soul.

Renunciation is not a wholly passive thing; it is not a mere suspicion of all that is joyful, a dull abnegation of happiness. It is not that self-sacrifice means a frame of mind too despondent to enjoy, so fearful of every kind of pleasure that it has not the heart to take part in it. It is rather a vigorous discrimination between pleasure and joy, an austerity which is not deceived by selfish, obvious, apparent pleasure, but sees what sort of pleasure is innocent, natural, social, and what sort of pleasure is corroding, barren, and unreal.

In the Christianity of the Gospel there is very little trace of asceticism. The delight in life is clearly indicated, and the only sort of self-denial that is taught is the self-denial that ends in simplicity of life, and in the joyful and courageous shouldering of inevitable burdens. Self-denial was not to be practised in a spiritless and timid way, but rather as a man accepts the fatigues and dangers of an expedition, in a vigorous and adventurous mood. One does not think of the men who go on some Arctic exploration, with all the restrictions of diet that they have to practise, all the uncomfortable rules of life they have to obey, as renouncing the joys of life; they do so naturally, in order that they may follow a livelier inspiration. It is clear from the accounts of primitive Christians that they impressed their heathen neighbours not as timid, anxious, and despondent people, but as men and women with some secret overflowing sense of joy and energy, and with a curious radiance and brightness about them which was not an affected pose, but the redundant happiness of those who have some glad knowledge in heart and mind which they cannot repress.

Let us suppose the case of a man gifted by nature with a great vitality, with a keen perception of all that is beautiful in life, all that is humorous, all that is delightful. Imagine him extremely sensitive to nature, art, human charm, human pleasure, doing everything with zest, interest, amusement, excitement. Imagine him, too, deeply sensitive to affection, loving to be loved, grateful, kindly, fond of children and animals, a fervent lover, a romantic friend, alive to all fine human qualities. Suppose, too, that he is ambitious, desirous of fame, liking to play an active part in life, fond of work, wishing to sway opinion, eager that others should care for the things for which he cares. Well, he must make a certain choice, no doubt; he cannot gratify all these things; his ambition may get in the way of his pleasure, his affections may interrupt his ambitions. What is his renunciation to be? It obviously will not be an abnegation of everything. He will not feel himself bound to crush all enjoyment, to refuse to love and be loved, to enter tamely and passively into life. He will inevitably choose what is dearest to his heart, whatever that may be, and he will no doubt instinctively eliminate from his life the joys which are most clouded by dissatisfaction. If he sets affection aside for the sake of ambition, and then finds that the thought of the love he has slighted or disregarded wounds and pains him, he will retrace his steps; if he sees that his ambitions leave him no time for his enjoyment of art or nature, and finds his success embittered by the loss of those other enjoyments, he will curb his ambition; but in all this he will not act anxiously and wretchedly. He will be rather like a man who has two simultaneous pleasures offered him, one of which must exclude the other. He will not spoil both, but take what he desires most, and think no more of what he rejects.

The more that such a man loves life, the less is he likely to be deceived by the shows of life; the more wisely will he judge what part of it is worth keeping, and the less will he be tempted by anything which distracts him from life itself. It is fulness of life, after all, that he is aiming at, and not vacuity; and thus renunciation becomes not a feeble withdrawal from life, but a vigorous affirmation of the worth of it.

But of course we cannot all expect to deal with life on this highhanded scale. The question is what most of us, who feel ourselves sadly limited, incomplete, fractious, discontented, fitful, unequal to the claims upon us, should do. If we have no sense of eager adventure, but are afraid of life, overshadowed by doubts and anxieties, with no great spring of pleasure, no passionate emotions, no very definite ambitions, what are we then to do?

Or perhaps our case is even worse than that; we are meanly desirous of comfort, of untroubled ease, we have a secret love of low pleasures, a desire to gain rather than to deserve admiration and respect, a temptation to fortify ourselves against life by accumulating all sorts of resources, with no particular wish to share anything, but aiming to be left alone in a circle which we can bend to our will and make useful to us; that is the hard case of many men and women; and even if by glimpses we see that there is a finer and a freer life outside, we may not be conscious of any real desire to issue from our stuffy parlour.

In either case our duty and our one hope is clear; that we have got somehow, at all costs and hazards, to find our way into the light of day. It is such as these, the anxious and the fearful on the one hand, the gross and sensual on the other, who need most of all a *Joyous Gard* of their own. Because we are coming to the light, as Walt Whitman so splendidly says: — "The Lord advances and yet advances . . . always the shadow in front, always the reach'd hand bringing up the laggards."

Our business, if we know that we are laggards, if we only dimly suspect it, is not to fear the shadow, but to seize the outstretched hands. We must grasp the smallest clue that leads out of the dark, the resolute fight with some slovenly and ugly habit, the telling of our mean troubles to some one whose energy we admire and whose disapproval we dread; we must try the experiment, make the plunge; all at once we realise that the foundations are laid, that the wall is beginning to rise above the rubbish and the débris; we must build a home for the new-found joy, even if as yet it only sings drowsily and faintly within our hearts, like the awaking bird in the dewy thicket, when the fingers of the dawn begin to raise the curtain of the night.

XXV
THE SENSE OF BEAUTY

There is one difficulty which stands at the threshold of dealing with the sense of beauty so as to give it due importance and preponderance, and that is that it seems with many people to be so frail a thing, and to visit the mind only as the last grace of a mood of perfect serenity and well-being. Many people, and those not the least thoughtful and intelligent, find by experience that it is almost the first thing to disappear in moments of stress and pressure. Physical pain, grief, pre-occupation, business, anxiety, all seem to have the power of quenching it instantaneously, until one is apt to feel that it is a thing of infinite delicacy and tenderness, and can only co-exist with a tranquillity which it is hard in life to secure. The result of this no doubt is that many active-minded and forcible people are ready to think little of it, and just regard it as a mood that may accompany a well-earned holiday, and even so to be sparingly indulged.

It is also undoubtedly true that in many robust and energetic people the sense of what is beautiful is so far atrophied that it can only be aroused by scenes and places of almost melodramatic picturesqueness, by ancient buildings clustered on craggy eminences, great valleys with the frozen horns of mountains, wind-ravaged and snow-streaked, peering over forest edges, the thunder and splendour of great sea-breakers plunging landward under rugged headlands and cliff-fronts. But all this pursuit of sensational beauty is to mistake its quality; the moment it is thus pursued it ceases to be the milk and honey of life, and it becomes a kind of stimulant which excites rather than tranquillises. I do not mean that one should of set purpose avoid the sight of wonderful prospects and treasure-houses of art, or act as the poet Gray did when he was travelling with Horace Walpole in the Alps, when they drew up the blinds of their carriage to exclude the sight of such prodigious and unmanning horrors!

Still I think that if one is on the right track, and if beauty has its due place and value in life, there will be less and less impulse to go far afield for it, in search of something to thrill the dull perception and quicken it into life. I believe that people ought to be content to live most of their lives in the same place, and to grow to love familiar scenes. Familiarity with a scene ought not to result in the obliteration of all consciousness of it: one ought rather to find in use and affection an increased power of subtle interpretation, a closer and finer understanding of the qualities which underlie the very simplest of English landscapes. I live, myself, for most of the year in a countryside that is often spoken of by its inhabitants as dull, tame, and featureless; yet I cannot say with what daily renewal of delight I wander in the pastoral Cambridge landscape, with its long low lines of wold, its whitewalled, straw-thatched villages embowered in orchards and elms, its slow willow-bound streams, its level fenland, with the far-seen cloud-banks looming overhead: or again in the high-ridged, well-wooded land of Sussex, where I often live, the pure lines of the distant downs seen over the richly coloured intervening weald grow daily more dear and intimate, and appeal more and more closely to the deepest secrets of sweetness and delight. For as we train ourselves to the perception of beauty, we become more and more alive to a fine simplicity of effect; we find the lavish accumulation of rich and magnificent glories bewildering and distracting.

And this is the same with other arts; we no longer crave to be dazzled and flooded by passionate and exciting sensation, we care less and less for studied mosaics of word and thought, and more and more for clearness and form and economy and austerity. Restless exuberance becomes unwelcome, complexity and intricacy weary us; we begin to perceive the beauty of what Fitzgerald called the 'great still books.' We do not desire a kaleidoscopic pageant of blending and colliding emotions, but crave for something distinctly seen, entirely grasped, perfectly developed. Because we are no longer in search of something stimulating and exciting, something to make us glide and dart among the surge and spray of life, but what we crave for is rather a calm and reposeful absorption in a thought which can yield us all its beauty, and assure us of the existence of a principle in which we can rest and abide. As life goes on, we ought not to find relief from tedium only in a swift interchange and multiplication of sensations; we ought rather to attain a simple and sustained joyfulness which can find nurture in homely and familiar things.

If again the sense of beauty is so frail a thing that it is at the mercy of all intruding and jarring elements, it is also one of the most patient and persistent of quiet forces. Like the darting fly which we scare from us, it returns again and again to settle on the spot which it has chosen. There are, it is true, troubled and anxious hours when the beauty round us seems a cruel and intrusive thing, mocking us with a peace which we cannot realise, and torturing us with the reminder of the joy we have lost. There are days when the only way to forget our misery is to absorb ourselves in some practical energy;

but that is because we have not learned to love beauty in the right way. If we have only thought of it as a pleasant ingredient in our cup of joy, as a thing which we can just use as we can use wine, to give us an added flush of unreasonable content, then it will fail us when we need it most. When a man is under the shadow of a bereavement, he can test for himself how he has used love. If he finds that the loving looks and words and caresses of those that are left to him are a mere torture to him, then he has used love wrongly, just as a selfish and agreeable delight; but if he finds strength and comfort in the yearning sympathy of friend and beloved, reassurance in the strength of the love that is left him, and confidence in the indestructibility of affection, then he has used love wisely and purely, loving it for itself, for its beauty and holiness, and not only for the warmth and comfort it has brought him.

So, if we have loved beauty well, have seen in it a promise of ultimate joy, a sign of a deliberate intention, a message from a power that does not send sorrow and anxiety wantonly, cruelly and indifferently, an assurance of something that waits to welcome and bless us, then beauty is not a mere torturing menace, a heartless and unkind parading of joy which we cannot feel, but a faithful pledge of something secure and everlasting, which will return to us again and again in ever fuller measure, even if the flow of it be sometimes suspended.

We ought then to train and practise our sense of beauty, not selfishly and luxuriously, but so that when the dark hour comes it may help us to realise that all is not lost, may alleviate our pain by giving us the knowledge that the darkness is the interruption, but that the joy is permanent and deep and certain.

Thus beauty, instead of being for us but as the melody swiftly played when our hearts are high, a mere momentary ray, a happy accident that befalls us, may become to us a deep and vital spring of love and hope, of which we may say that it is there waiting for us, like the home that awaits the traveller over the weary upland at the foot of the far-looming hill. It may come to us as a perpetual sign that we are not forgotten, and that the joy of which it makes mention survives all interludes of strife and uneasiness. It is easy to slight and overlook it, but if we do that, we are deluded by the passing storm into believing that confusion and not peace is the end. As George Meredith nobly wrote, during the tragic and fatal illness of his wife, "Here I am in the very pits of tragic life. . . . Happily for me, I have learnt to live much in the spirit, and see brightness on the other side of life, otherwise this running of my poor doe with the inextricable arrow in her flanks would pull me down too."

The spirit, the brightness of the other side, that is the secret which beauty can communicate, and the message which she bears upon her radiant wings.

XXVI
THE PRINCIPLE OF BEAUTY

"I have loved," said Keats, "the *principle* of beauty in all things." It is that to which all I have said has been leading, as many roads unite in one. We must try to use discrimination, not to be so optimistic that we see beauty if it is not there, not to overwhelm every fling that every craftsman has at beauty with gush and panegyric; not to praise beauty in all companies, or to go off like a ripe broom-pod, at a touch. When Walter Pater was confronted with something which courtesy demanded that he should seem to admire, he used to say in that soft voice of his, which lingered over emphatic syllables, "Very costly, no doubt!"

But we must be generous to all beautiful intention, and quick to see any faintest beckoning of the divine quality; and indeed I would not have most people aim at too critical an attitude, for I believe it is more important to enjoy than to appraise; still we must keep the principle in sight, and not degenerate into mere collectors of beautiful impressions. If we simply try to wallow in beauty, we are using it sensually; while if on the other hand we aim at correctness of taste, which is but the faculty of sincere concurrence with the artistic standards of the day, we come to a sterile connoisseurship which has no living inspiration about it. It is the temperate use of beauty which we must aim at, and a certain candour of observation, looking at all things, neither that we may condemn if we can, nor that we may luxuriously abandon ourselves to sensation, but that we may draw from contemplation something of the inner light of life.

I have not here said much about the arts — music, sculpture, painting, architecture — because I do not want to recommend any specialisation in beauty. I know, indeed, several high-minded people, diligent, unoriginal, faithful, who have begun by recognising in a philosophical way the worth and force of beauty, but who, having no direct instinct for it, have bemused themselves by conventional and conscientious study, into the belief that they are on the track of beauty in art, when they have no real appreciation of it at all, no appetite for it, but are only bent on perfecting temperament, and whose unconscious motive has been but a fear of not being in sympathy with men whose ardour they admire, but whose love of beauty they do not really share. Such people tend to gravitate to early Italian painting, because of its historical associations, and because it can be categorically studied. They become what is called 'purists,' which means little more than a learned submissiveness. In literature they are found to admire Carlyle, Ruskin, and Browning, not because of their method of treating thought, but because of the ethical maxims imbedded — as though one were to love a conserve of plums for the sake of the stones!

One should love great writers and great artists not because of their great thoughts — there are plenty of inferior writers who traffic in great thoughts — but because great artists and writers are the people who can irradiate with a heavenly sort of light common thoughts and motives, so as to show the beauty which underlies them and the splendour that breaks from them. It is possible to treat fine thoughts in a heavy way so as to deprive them of all their rarity and inspiration. The Gospel contains some of the most beautiful thoughts in the world, beautiful because they are common thoughts which every one recognises to be true, yet set in a certain light, just as the sunset with its level, golden, remote glow has the power of transfiguring a familiar scene with a glory of mystery and desire. But one has but to turn over a volume of dull sermons, or the pages of a dreary commentary, to find the thoughts of the Gospel transformed into something that seems commonplace and uninspiring. The beauty of ordinary things depends upon the angle at which you see them and the light which falls upon them; and the work of the great artist and the great writer is to show things at the right angle, and to shut off the confusing muddled cross-lights which conceal the quality of the thing seen.

The recognition of the principle of beauty lies in the assurance that many things have beauty, if rightly viewed, and in the determination to see things in the true light. Thus the soul that desires to see beauty must begin by believing it to be there, must expect to see it, must watch for it, must not be discouraged by those who do not see it, and least of all give heed to those who would forbid one to discern it except in definite and approved forms. The worst of æsthetic prophets is that, like the Scribes, they make a fence about the law, and try to convert the search for principle into the accumulation of detailed tenets.

Let us then never attempt to limit beauty to definite artistic lines; that is the mistake of the superstitious formalist who limits divine influences to certain sanctuaries and fixed ceremonials. The use of the sanctuary and the ceremonial is only to concentrate at one fiery point the wide current of impulsive ardour. The true lover of beauty will await it everywhere, will see it in the town, with its rising roofs and its bleached and blackened steeples, in the seaport with its quaint crowded shipping, in the clustered hamlet with its orchard-closes and high-roofed barns, in the remote country with its wide fields and its converging lines, in the beating of the sea on shingle-bank and promontory; and then if he sees it there, he will see it concentrated and emphasised in pictures of these things, the beauty of which lies so often in the sense of the loving apprehension of the mystery of lights and hues; and then he will trace the same subtle spirit in the forms and gestures and expressions of those among whom he lives, and will go deeper yet and trace the same spirit in conduct and behaviour, in the free and gallant handling of life, in the suppression of mean personal desires, in doing dull and disagreeable things with a fine end in view, in the noble affection of the simplest people; until he becomes aware that it is a quality which runs through everything he sees or hears or feels, and that the eternal difference is whether one views things dully and stupidly, regarding the moment hungrily and greedily, as a dog regards a plateful of food, or whether one looks at it all as a process which has some fine and distant end in view, and sees that all experience, whether it be of things tangible and visible, or of things intellectual and spiritual, is only precious because it carries one forward, forms, moulds, and changes one with a hope of some high and pure resurrection out of things base and hurried into things noble and serene.

The need, the absolute need for all and each of us, is to find something strong and great to rest and repose upon. Otherwise one simply falls back on the fact that one exists and on the whole enjoys existing, while one shuns the pain and darkness of ceasing to exist. As life goes on, there comes such an impulse to say, "Life is attractive and might be pleasant, but there is always something shadowing it, spoiling it, gnawing at it, a worm in the bud, of which one cannot be rid." And so one sinks into a despairing apathy.

What then is one born for? Just to live and forget, to be hurt and healed, to be strong and grow weak? That as the spirit falls into faintness, the body should curdle into worse than dust? To give each a memory of things sharp and sweet, that no one else remembers, and then to destroy that?

No, that is not the end! The end is rather to live fully and ardently, to recognise the indestructibility of the spirit, to strip off from it all that wounds and disables it, not by drearily toiling against haunting faults, but by rising as often as we can into serene ardour and deep hopefulness. That is the principle of beauty, to feel that there is something transforming and ennobling us, which we can lay hold of if we wish, and that every time we see the great spirit at work and clasp it close to our feeble will, we soar a step higher and see all things with a wider and a clearer vision.

XXVII
LIFE

But in all this, and indeed beyond all this, we must not dare to forget one thing; that it is life with which we are confronted, and that our business is to live it, and to live it in our own way; and here we may thankfully rejoice that there is less and less tendency in the world for people to dictate modes of life to us; the tyrant and the despot are not only out of date — they are out of fashion, which is a far more disabling thing! There is of course a type of person in the world who loves to call himself robust and even virile — heaven help us to break down that bestial ideal of manhood! — who is of the stuff that all bullies have been made since the world began, a compound of courage, stupidity, and complacency; to whom the word 'living' has no meaning, unless it implies the disturbing and disquieting of other people. We are gradually putting him in his right place, and the kindlier future will have little need of him; because a sense is gradually shaping itself in the world that life is best lived on peaceful and orderly lines.

But if the robust *viveur* is on the wrong tack, so long as he grabs and uses, and neither gives nor is used, so too the more peaceable and poetical nature makes a very similar mistake, if his whole heart is bent upon receiving and enjoying; for he too is filching and conveying away pleasure out of life, though he may do it more timidly and unobtrusively. Such a man or woman is apt to make too much out of the occasions and excitements of life, to over-value the æsthetic kind of success, which is the delicate impressing of other people, claiming their admiration and applause, and being ill-content if one is not noticed and praised. Such an one is apt to overlook the common stuff and use of life — the toil, the endurance, the discipline of it; to flutter abroad only on sunshiny days, and to sit sullenly with folded wing when the sky breaks into rain and chilly winds are blowing. The man who lives thus, is in danger of overvaluing the raptures and thrills of life, of being fitful and moody and fretful; what he has to do is to spread serenity over his days, and above all to be ready to combine, to minister, to sympathise, to serve. *Joyous Gard* is a very perilous place, if we grow too indolent to leave it; the essence of it is refreshment and not continuance. There are two conditions attached to the use of it; one is that we should have our own wholesome work in the world, and the second that we should not grow too wholly absorbed in labour.

No great moral leaders and inspirers of men have ever laid stress on excessive labour. They have accepted work as one of the normal conditions of life, but their whole effort has been to teach men to look away from work, to find leisure to be happy and good. There is no essential merit in work, apart from its necessity. Of course men may find themselves in positions where it seems hard to avoid a fierce absorption in work. It is said by legislators that the House of Commons, for instance, is a place where one can neither work nor rest! And I have heard busy men in high administrative office, deplore rhetorically the fact that they have no time to read or think. It is almost as unwholesome never to read or think as it is to be always reading and thinking, because the light and the inspiration fade out of life, and leave one a gaunt and wolfish lobbyist, who goes about seeking whom he may indoctrinate. But I have little doubt that when the world is organised on simpler lines, we shall look back to this era, as an era when men's heads were turned by work, and when more unnecessary things were made and done and said than has ever been the case since the world began.

The essence of happy living is never to find life dull, never to feel the ugly weariness which comes of overstrain; to be fresh, cheerful, leisurely, sociable, unhurried, well-balanced. It seems to me that it is impossible to be these things unless we have time to consider life a little, to deliberate, to select, to abstain. We must not help ourselves either to work or to joy as if we were helping ourselves to potatoes! If life ought not to be perpetual drudgery, neither can it be a perpetual feast. What I believe we ought to aim at is to put interest and zest into the simplest acts, words, and relations of life, to discern the quality of work and people alike. We must not turn our whole minds and hearts to literature or art or work, or even to religion; but we must go deeper, and look close at life itself, which these interpret and out of which they flow. For indeed life is nobler and richer than any one interpretation of it. Let us take for a moment one of the great interpreters of life, Robert Browning, who was so intensely interested above all things in personality. The charm of his writing is that he contrives, by some fine instinct, to get behind and within the people of whom he writes, sees with their eyes, hears with their ears, though he speaks with his own lips. But one must observe that the judgment of none of his characters is a final judgment; the artist, the lover, the cynic, the charlatan, the sage, the priest — they none of them provide a solution to life; they set out on their quest, they make their guesses, they reveal their aims, but they never penetrate the inner secret. It is all inference and hope; Browning himself seems to believe in life, not because of the reasons which his characters give for believing in it, but in spite of all their reasons. Like little boats, the reasons seem to strand, one by one, some sooner, some later, on the sands beneath the shallow sea; and then the great serene large faith of the poet comes flooding in, and bears them on their way.

It is somewhat thus that we must deal with life; it is no good making up a philosophy which just keeps us gay when all is serene and prosperous. Unpleasant, tedious, vexing, humiliating, painful, shattering things befall us all by the way. That is the test of our belief in life, if nothing daunts us, if nothing really mars our serenity of mood.

And so what this little book of mine tries to recommend is that we should bestir ourselves to design, plan, use, practise life; not drift helplessly on its current, shouting for joy when all is bright, helplessly bemoaning ourselves when all is dark; and that we should do this by guarding ourselves from impulse and whim, by feeding our minds and hearts on all the great words, high examples, patient endurances, splendid acts, of those whom we recognise to have been the finer sort of men. One of the greatest blessings of our time is that we can do that so easily. In the dullest, most monotonous life we can stay ourselves upon this heavenly manna, if we have the mind. We need not feel alone or misunderstood or unappreciated, even if we are surrounded by harsh, foolish, dry, discontented, mournful persons. The world is fuller now than it ever was of brave and kindly people who will help us if we ask for help. Of course if we choose to perish without a struggle, we can do that. And my last word of advice to people into whose hands this book may fall, who are suffering from a sense of dim failure, timid bewilderment, with a vague desire in the background to make something finer and stronger out of life, is to turn to some one whom they can trust — not intending to depend constantly and helplessly upon them — and to get set in the right road.

Of course, as I have said, care and sorrow, heaviness and sadness — even disillusionment — must come; but the reason of that is because we must not settle too close to the sweet and kindly earth, but be ready to unfurl our wings for the passage over sea; and to what new country of God, what unknown troops and societies of human spirits, what gracious reality of dwelling-place, of which our beloved fields and woods and streams are nothing but the gentle and sweet symbols, our flight may bear us, I cannot tell; but that we are all in the mind of God, and that we cannot wander beyond the reach of His hand or the love of His heart, of this I am more sure than I am of anything else in this world where familiarity and mystery are so strangely entwined.

THE END

www.ingramcontent.com/pod-product-compliance
Lightning Source LLC
LaVergne TN
LVHW011209080426
835508LV00007B/696